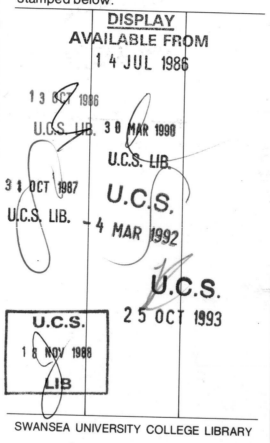

SOLDIER, SOLDIER

Books by Tony Parker

The Courage of His Convictions
The Unknown Citizen
The Plough Boy
Five Women
A Man of Good Abilities
People of the Streets
The Twisting Lane: Some Sex Offenders
The Frying Pan: A Prison and Its Prisoners
In No Man's Land: Some Unmarried Mothers
The Man Inside (ed.)
Three Television Plays
Lighthouse
The People of Providence: A Housing Estate and
    Some of Its Inhabitants

SOLDIER, SOLDIER

Tony Parker

HEINEMANN : LONDON

William Heinemann Ltd
10 Upper Grosvenor Street, London WIX 9PA
LONDON MELBOURNE TORONTO
JOHANNESBURG AUCKLAND

First published 1985
© Tony Parker 1985
SBN 434 57770 7

Photoset in Great Britain by
Rowland Phototypesetting Ltd, Bury St Edmunds, Suffolk
Printed and bound by Mackays of Chatham,
Chatham, Kent

For Rachel and Isaac
with love

And for The Vikings, The Poachers and The Pompadours with
great respect

The sweet war man is dead and
rotten; sweet chucks, beat not
the bones of the buried. When
he breathed, he was a man.

Love's Labour's Lost, V, ii

Their stricken bones lie all about the world,
Who were my friends in England; and the law
Permits me to have loved them, who lack flesh.

Eyes winked, once, in the skull. Ribs that are curled
Under the sand, under the sea, under the hairy paw
Of Death who sent the flies, who sent the fish,
Had once a heart. Pluck me that heart, now . . .

For these bare bones were children, when they died.

Paul Dehn: *The Fern on the Rock*

Contents

1   Overtures and Beginners   1

2   Three Lives   9

   i.   A smashing life: George Bennett, private   11
   ii. A thoroughly enjoyable life: Richard Johnson,
        commanding officer   14
   iii. A not too bad life: Valerie Miller, corporal's wife   16

3   Some of the Lads   21

   i.   Keeping your nose clean: Chalky White, private   23
   ii. Hell and fucks: Billy The Kid, private   25
   iii. Having thoughts: Dongo Bell, private   28
   iv. Planning it all out: Ginger Jim, private   30

4   And We in the Meantime   35

   i.   Back home in somewhere: Ingrid Wilson, private's
        wife   37
   ii. Racketing about: Jenny Donald, lance corporal's
        wife   40
   iii. One tries one's best: Philippa Jordan, captain's wife 43

5   Voices of Experience   47

   i.   An enormous amount of sense: Adrian Allen,
        second lieutenant   49
   ii. All the worrying: Peter Jones, captain   52
   iii. A killing machine: John Taylor, major   56

6   Forwards, Sideways, Backwards   59

    i.   Keeping up with going up: Mary York, sergeant's
          wife   61
    ii.   Finding time to be me: Julia Clark, lieutenant's wife   64
    iii. Right in the shit: Audrey Brown, private's wife   67

7   No Problem   71

    i.   The tallest man in town: Geoff Marshall, private   73
    ii.   Going out of my way: Joseph Smith, corporal   75
    iii. Wait till you see me chick: Jack Green, sergeant   77
    iv.   Having a quiet laugh: Roger Dawson, staff sergeant   79

8   Up through the Ranks   81

    i.   Never in my wildest: Tom Edwards, captain   83
    ii.   Conservative Conservative: Walter Davies,
          lieutenant   87
    iii. Taking the Queen's shilling: Bert Price, major   90

9   People like Us   95

    i.   Honoured by service: Harold Harrison, major   97
    ii.   Young Lochinvar: David Jenkins, major   100
    iii. I'm your man sir: Douglas Gibson, lance corporal   103
    iv.   Me and my brothers: Kevin Bishop, private   105

10 Number One Top Soldier   109

    i.   The Pinnacle: Charles Thompson, RSM   111
    ii.   Charlie Chase   114
    iii. Person to person: Mrs Thompson   117

11 In Several Places   121

    i.   Germany   123
    ii.   Belize   128
    iii. Cyprus   138
    iv.   England   145

12 A Totally Different Country   155

13 At the Edge of the Common   175

    i.   Idiots without brains: Andrew Nash, second
          lieutenant   177
    ii.   Thinking the unthinkable: Donald Morris,
          lieutenant   179

iii.   All those selfish bitches: Susan Shaw, private's wife   181
iv.   Utterable contempt: Jennifer Long, captain's wife   184
v.   And furthermore   186

14   In Command: The General   191

15   Soldier, Soldier   199

16   In Ordinary Life   213

i.   Boxes: Harry Roberts, furniture dealer   215
ii.   What I am now: Norman Jackson, stable manager   219
iii.   Please God don't let it happen: Cathy Harper,
       secretary   223
iv.   No sort of a job: Malcolm Grant, unemployed   227

17   Coda: The Sweet War Man   231

Acknowledgments   242

1   Overtures and Beginners

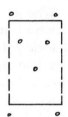

They call it a brick. As they move slowly along the street of wrecked terraced houses, the two soldiers right and left at the front swing their automatic rifles threateningly from side to side. Their eyes scan the broken windows, the boarded doorways, the rooftops, each crossroad and street corner coming up ahead. The two other soldiers left and right at the rear do the same, walking backwards.

Between them in the middle on the left the tall young lieutenant strolls nonchalantly, as though to display his contempt for danger: he chats quietly in his public school drawl about the gusting cold wind and the increasingly heavy drizzle and what a frightfully lousy winter it's been. His pistol stays in its holster, but he keeps his hand thumb-hooked in his camouflage field-jacket pocket near it. Behind him the sergeant's eyes and rifle are swivelling ceaselessly forwards, sideways, upwards, backwards. "Christ not Ipswich Town?" he says out of the corner of his mouth with a mock-disbelieving laugh. "You don't really support them do you, a bunch of wankers like that?" A Norfolk man, must be.

Anyone watching through binoculars or a telescopic sight, seeing the small portly hatless civilian in a raincoat on the lieutenant's right, would think surely he's of at least some importance, so heavily guarded and protected like he is? Worth a pot shot, or perhaps even a lobbed grenade in the general direction of?

I'm not happy about it. What do I think I'm doing, I'm asking

myself – an ageing pacifist, a conscientious objector in the 1939–45
war, walking surrounded by armed men like this down the middle
of a derelict Londonderry street on a dark wet January afternoon?

"Please Sam don't forget my principles," I say to the sergeant.
"You know I don't want anyone killed on my behalf." "Don't you
worry mate," he says with a grin. "We won't kill them on your
behalf, we'll do it on behalf of the British Army."

(notebook)

Memo to Tony Parker re possible non-fiction book

We would like you to consider the idea of doing a book about the
contemporary British Army. Who joins the Army and why? How
does the Army work as a society? Is its system of values different
from that of the rest of British society? Does it have any tacit or open
political leanings? How does joining the Army affect soldiers'
domestic lives? These questions and many more might be explored
in a book of tape-recorded interviews. The aim would be to find a
particular regiment which would allow you the freedom of access to
its members, from the colonel to raw recruits. Your own background as a conscientious objector would, we suggest, lead you to
ask some significant questions, and perhaps see the answers in a
different perspective from that of other writers.

(Charles Clark, publisher)

It has been suggested to me that since conscription no longer exists,
most people have little idea what the British Army is now like in
human terms – what sort of people become soldiers and why, how
they see themselves, how in turn they look on society. And that the
idea of a pacifist and World War II conscientious objector trying to
interview them and find out might produce a result which could be
unusual. That's if the Army would even for one moment consider it.

I live in Suffolk, so it seems natural first to approach my "local"
regiment, the Royal Anglians: a traditional infantry regiment, a
"regiment of the line".

I've met and talked with some of the Royal Anglians' senior
officers and with Ministry of Defence officials in London, to explain
what I hope to do and how. To my astonishment I was very rapidly
given permission, and offered complete co-operation and widespread facilities by everyone. I made it clear what my own attitudes
and prejudices were, and have repeatedly done so whoever
I've talked to. I have to say I've never been treated by a single

person with anything other than courtesy, helpfulness, and open friendliness.

(notebook)

The infantryman is generally of supreme importance because he holds the territory. The Royal Air Force may pound it to pulp, the Artillery may reduce it to ashes, the Royal Navy may fight tremendous battles at sea and transport troops to maintain the lifelines, but the infantry holds the ground or takes territory.

(Captain Edgar Letts: "Tracing the Regiments")

On arrival, tea in the officers' mess: a welcoming warm comfortably furnished room with big armchairs, lots of settees, military oil paintings. and mounted and framed medals and decorations all round the walls. About thirty officers. Toast, cake, chatter. "How do you do, how very nice to meet you, it's good to have you with us. I am the commanding officer, I shall call you Tony and you must call me Julian. I do hope you enjoy your stay with us."

(notebook)

– I hope your book won't only contain interviews with highly motivated soldiers and no one else: that'd give a very false picture. But it's going to be difficult to avoid it, because we have an all-volunteer Army. If a man's really unhappy we don't want to keep him, and he doesn't have to stay. So nearly all the people you talk to are going to tell you they're happy, the Army's a wonderful organization, and they want to go on and on being soldiers. By the mere fact of them still being in the Army, they mostly do think and feel that. So this'll really be a big difficulty for you.

(L.M., commanding officer)

– I think it would be something worth doing if it contained a true account, or as near a true account as one could get, of how we live: it might be painful and embarrassing in parts, indeed I think it wouldn't be honest or worth doing if it wasn't. But perhaps you might show us as not entirely stereotypes, not just mechanical men who obey orders and don't think.

(Eric C., lieutenant)

– Perhaps you could help people understand the amount of intellect that is necessary in the Army. A soldier has to be a counter-terrorist fighter in the streets of Northern Ireland, almost something of a guerilla fighter: then out and out aggressive on some such occasion as the Falklands war, then a diplomat when he's with the United Nations forces in Cyprus, and finally just a member of a visiting Army – certainly not an "occupying" army – when he's in Germany. Equally he gets moved from one climate to another from one country to another, and is expected to acclimatize both physically and mentally very quickly. Civilian life makes no such demands that are even comparable on people.

(Dennis B., major)

– I sometimes think, you know, that being a soldier is a kind of fate. But surely you can't be picked out like that? I mean well I hope you can't. Sometimes I think being a soldier isn't really worthwhile at all – but I find it very hard to think what else I could do. You see I come from an Army family: and though neither my father nor anyone else ever put pressure on me, it was always taken for granted I was going in the Army. So – here I am at the age of twenty-six, in the Army. But sometimes I don't think I've ever even been able to make a free choice for myself about it.

(Robert T., captain)

– The challenge of leadership, the responsibility of leadership: that'd be worth including. I mean if you're a platoon commander you're responsible for about 30 men, if you're a company commander it's about 100 men – and if you're the commanding officer of a battalion, it's 600 to 1,000 men. I mean wow.

(Jonathan D., second lieutenant)

– As a commanding officer of one of the companies, there're a lot of things I'd like to ask soldiers but can't. I wonder to what extent Army life is a refuge to some, a sort of escape from the real world outside. What they really think about the life they have, that sort of thing. How they feel about what you might call the 'servant–master' set-up between officers and other ranks . . . it'd be interesting to ask other ranks, and to ask officers.

Chat with everyone you can – some of the lads, some young officers and old ones, listen to their voices of experience – everyone you possibly can. And I do hope you end up with something which isn't only about the glorification of the Army – in its own eyes, or what it thinks or hopes is the public's eyes either. That'd be very dull. Try for a realistic cross-section giving all sides.

(Paul T., major)

— I'd say the strongest influence on whether a man is a good – in the sense of successful and happy – soldier is his marital situation. If he's married a woman who is a soldier's wife, in all the possible meanings of the phrase, then he'll be OK. So your book shouldn't ignore this, it's a vitally important factor of Army life: in fact I'd say you should devote quite a lot of time to talking to wives, both happy ones and unhappy ones, and trying to get their views. Their views are very often overlooked, ignored as unimportant, and so something might be done to redress that balance.

(Peter W., captain)

— Your book might damage us if it contains too many of your own misperceptions. You perhaps might not interview enough people, or you could select and edit your interviews in such a way as to give a very unbalanced picture. You must get all different ranks represented, all different types of person from different backgrounds with different experiences. You won't get it, but you should at least try to get a total feel – not just mad keen soldiers but some less keen ones too. And not all Hooray Henrys either: there are some, there are bound to be, just as you would find people like that in any walk of society. But I hope no one type will be over-represented.

(Simon P., captain)

— I think it's a very good idea for you to be doing this book – and please tell your publishers also that I think it's a good idea. I feel it will allow soldiers to express something about themselves to an independent observer, which will then come to the eyes of the British public. And I believe it will illustrate to the public that the imagery of say the 1930s is long dead. The image was probably always too stark and false in a number of ways – the Colonel Blimp image, the idea of the unthinking soldier, the idea of an Army that actually lived inwards. Because what we have today is an Army for the twenty-first century – very much aware of its glorious past – and not all of it that glorious too – and we have been a marvellous servant for this country and will continue to be so. In many ways we set an example, as we do now in terms of the way we live together as people respecting each other. I deeply respect the men I lead, and I'm confident I won't let them down nor will they let me down. And I think society in the country as a whole might just copy that a little, and then we might get a rebirth of national happiness, which doesn't seem too apparent at the moment. I think society's got a

very great deal to learn about life from its Army – so that's why I
think it's a good idea.

(General T.)

It seems to me already by now early on that rather than having a
book of one-off "public relations" interviews, I should try to get to
know a small number of soldiers, and also some of their wives, so
we can talk unhurriedly and at length. Also I feel it might help me try
and understand the nature of their life better, and them perhaps to
regard me as less of a remote observer, if I can on occasions spend
time with them on some of the postings that they experience. So I've
asked for and been given permission to talk with the same soldiers
not only in their barracks in the UK, but also in Northern Ireland, in
the Belize jungle, in Cyprus with the United Nations, in Seattle USA
on exercise, and in Germany with the British Army of the Rhine.

(notebook)

– The main pitfall I think you should look out for is not seeing that
the Army is very diverse: so a picture of it as entirely uniform in
every sense would be wrong. A great deal depends on the selection
of people you make, and what prominence you give to whose
opinions. Another problem might be that some men, of all ranks,
really revel in the thought of being 'a typical soldier'. To me, if
anyone called me that, I would regard it as an insult, it's like
someone trying to put a big rubber stamp on you. But not everyone
reacts in that way.

(Hugh R., lieutenant)

– To me definitely weaponry and uniforms don't make the Army, so
I'd like to see a sort of anthology of people, people in a national
institution and with warts and all. Some of the warts? Well, the
press sometimes criticize the toughness of our attitudes in certain
circumstances, and say we are being harder on people than we need
to be. Well not all our soldiers are angels, so perhaps that's one
wart. Another might be that you'd find parts of our social organization, our structural culture, a bit narrow. Elitism is, I should think,
one of the things you'll very quickly notice and perhaps find fault
with: I'd well understand any outsider who thought we behaved too
much as though we considered ourselves an elite. But all in all I'd
hope you gave a fair all-round picture.

(Phillip M., commanding officer)

2   Three Lives

i.   *A smashing life:*
       George Bennett, private

ii.   *A thoroughly enjoyable life:*
       Richard Johnson, commanding
       officer

iii.   *A not too bad life:*
       Valerie Miller, corporal's wife

i. A smashing life: George Bennett, private

— Can't think of anything I'd like to do better no, matter of fact I've always been what they call Army barmy. Ever since I was a kid at school there's been nothing else I've wanted to do. I was always playing the games, war games, fighting and that, I mean around the streets and places, where we lived. It was a town in Lincolnshire: I think I must have been about eleven or something about that, and one day I saw these soldiers marching through the town. I was standing watching with my Mum: I said to her "I'm going to be one of them one day." She said to me "You'll be lucky," she said, "you'll have to grow a bit first." Well I was lucky I reckon, because I did grow a bit and I did get into the Army, so here I am. It's a smashing life. At the moment I'm signed on for nine year, but if I still feel like I do now then I shall sign on for ninety-nine more. The way I see it, the Army suits me and I suit the Army, and I hope it goes on like that.

I'm nearly nineteen, well I'll be nineteen next week. I've been in two and a half years so far, I was just gone sixteen when I joined. I didn't have no exams or things when I left school: I took a couple of CSEs but I didn't get them. I didn't know what to do when I left so I mucked around for a bit. I started on a brick-laying course but my heart wasn't in it, and I had a job for a few weeks stacking shelves in a supermarket. Dead boring and it didn't seem I was getting anywhere.

I don't come from an Army family. My Dad had been in for his National Service, but after that he went on to factory work, something like that. He's the sort that's always been a rolling stone, never settled down to anything much. To be honest with you, I don't think he and my Mum've hit it off all that well a long time now. There were plenty of times Dad wasn't living at home: at the beginning I remember my Mum used to cry about it. I think he might've been off with other women and things: Mum told me and my sister he was away working. Then after a bit she didn't seem to bother. There were times when he was living in the house, there were times when he wasn't: that was how it was, mostly. My sister is older than me: she got married very early, not long after she was sixteen. There was a baby on the way probably I should think, because now she's got three kids already.

When she left home that left just me and my Mum on our own. It wasn't bad, but it was a dull sort of life. Where we lived was a small village on the edge of the town, you had to take a long bus ride if you wanted to go anywhere to do shopping or things like that. All the time I had this idea in my mind I'd like to go in the Army: but at first I thought when I left school I ought to try and help out at home and Mum would want me to stay. I told her I'd joined up and it's ironical when I think about it: there was this feller she'd got, and they were waiting for me to move out of the house for him to move in. He was quite a decent sort of bloke with a steady job, he was a long distance road driver: he gives my Mum a much better sort of life than my Dad ever did. I've not seen my Dad for quite a few years now. I don't know whether they've divorced or not, I think it's just one of those arrangements people have. When I go home on leave Ted – that's my Mum's bloke – he's there all the time, he and I go out and have a drink together, we get on OK. I think it was not having much of a home life that probably stood me in good stead when I come in the Army. By that I mean I was able to stand on my own feet and look after myself and be independent and that sort of thing.

In the town there was an Army recruiting shop in one of the main streets. I just went in there and had a bit of a talk with them, and they gave me some little tests. I passed those without any trouble, then I had to go to Harrogate for three days. There was another centre there where they gave you some more tests: not just written ones, but a few practical ones too. Then they said to go home and wait, I'd be hearing from them. I'd almost given up hope before I did hear, because I think it was nearly six months: then I got the letter which told me to report to the depot at Bassingbourne, and meant I'd been accepted, I had a talk with Mum and Ted, and he said there'd be good times and bad times, but if I could stick it out I'd make a go of it. My Mum was a bit worried because I'd never lived away from home: I think she thought I might be lonely.

When you go to the depot, the first thing they do is give you a good beasting. That means they shout at you and bawl at you, make you run around or stand out in the freezing cold on the parade ground for hours, generally treat you like shit. The idea is that if you can stand up to that, then you're on your way to be a soldier. They won't let you go out of the place: and at night you're so tired all you want to do is drop on your bed anyway. You don't get no privacy, and you're generally made to feel you're no good as a person at all. They get you up at half past six in the dark and make you go out and run, and they're all the time breathing down your neck and cursing and swearing at you.

After two weeks I was feeling I couldn't put up with it any longer. I wanted to be a soldier but they were telling me all the time I'd never make it because I hadn't got it in me. I rang my Mum up, and I said I was homesick and I was going to come home and have another think about it. She said if I did that the Army'd not let me back in again, that was the whole idea of what they were doing. She must have known more about it than she let on, because the only thing I'd said was homesick, I'd not told her anything about the rough side of it. Anyway she said try it a bit longer.

You have to stay six weeks before they give you leave, then you can go home for a few days. They must have it all worked out very carefully, because when my six weeks was up and I went home I was well over the worst. In fact I was boasting a bit about how tough it had been, but how I'd been able to take everything they did to me and still come up smiling. That was a bit of an exaggeration, because I often wasn't smiling very much. There was this sergeant major who if he ever saw you looking amused about anything, he'd roar at you "I'll soon get that fucking smile off your fucking face my lad." But the other thing is that after that period of time, the six weeks, you're beginning to feel you've got mates among the other lads who are in it with you. So when I went home I was even quite looking forward to going back again if you understand what I mean.

After you've done your year at the depot, then you really feel you're starting to be a soldier. You're what they call a Junior Soldier until you're eighteen, and there are certain things you can't do. You get treated as a bit of a teaboy: wherever you are, you're just a servant. You have to make tea for whoever tells you to, and sweep out offices and corridors and things. But once that's over, then they've got other younger boys coming in and you get given a bit of respect.

I don't mind where I go, they can send me where they like. That's what I joined for, to travel to places and see the world. I'm looking forward to Northern Ireland, Belize, Cyprus, Germany – all the places the battalion's going to or's going back to, and I know I shall enjoy it. The thing I like best of all is the fitness side, the adventure training and sports things, they're the best part of it. That and the mates you make, they're a good part of it too. I don't have a regular girlfriend, and I don't think I will have for quite a bit yet. I've had a few girls and that, but nothing serious. When I go home, some of the girls in the village seem a lot more keen on going out with a soldier than they used to be when I knew them before. But of course a soldier's got a regular job and the money isn't too bad, so I suppose there's that side of it for them to consider.

I can't say there's very much about it I don't like, because I enjoy most of it nearly all the time. Soldiering to me is about being a soldier, wearing a uniform and being on exercises, carrying your pack and your rifle and sleeping in holes in the ground or running around and learning how to fight people. After your first year or two you find out whether you can do it or not, and whether it's the sort of life for you. It is for me, there's no question about that, and I'd like to stay in and perhaps get as high as full corporal. That's my ambition.

ii. *A thoroughly enjoyable life: Richard Johnson, commanding officer*

– I am myself the son of a soldier: but my father was very conscious of possible dangers if he pushed me into the Army. He'd seen it happen with quite a few senior officers' sons, that they'd followed their father's profession somewhat unthinkingly, had been totally unsuitable for the Army or indeed any form of service life, had not made a success of their careers, and had grown up to be rather unhappy because such high expectations had been put on them.

When I was at school I remember that for a time I wanted to be a lawyer. But I was in the Cadet Corps and I liked that very much: and when the opportunity came to go with the Corps on a trip to Sandhurst to see what it was like, I very much liked what I saw. So that was what finally decided me to try and become a soldier. When I told my father, he was keen I should have some kind of fallback, and suggested I went in the Engineers and got a degree. But I failed to take his advice, and joined the Infantry without the benefit of a university education. It's certainly not something I've ever regretted: I went straight from school into Sandhurst, I've been in the Army by now for over twenty-one years, and it's the only job I've ever had. I intend to spend the rest of my working life doing it, and stay in until I'm fifty-five or they decide to throw me out.

I'm quite sure I did the right thing in not following one of my original inclinations for being a lawyer. I enjoy physical activity and travel, and I'd have been very bored I think by that kind of a career. And of course I'd travelled a great deal during my early years, having been with my father and family to Kenya, Malaya, Cyprus, South Africa and so on. There was always the excitement of looking forward to the next place one was going to be living in. In retrospect I think I assessed myself absolutely correctly in deciding that this would be the right life for me.

I went to Sandhurst at eighteen and spent two years there: then I left and joined this battalion as a second lieutenant. My first posting was to Aden, where soon after my arrival – though not in any way connected with it if I may say so – the troubles began. After that I came back to England for a course on small arms, then I went to Germany where I had my first platoon commander's position. I then went to the battalion depot at Bury St Edmunds, where I was for two and a half years: then I got married there. Let me see, what came next: yes, to Catterick where I was 2 I/C of a company. That was followed by my first tour in Northern Ireland, where I was a captain and the battalion adjutant. Then Cyprus on a two-year posting, and after that I went to the Ministry of Defence as a staff officer.

Although I'd dreaded the prospect of pen pushing, in fact I enjoyed it greatly and found the work fascinating. After that I went to the Staff College at Camberley and then came back to the battalion as major and a company commander. Back to Germany after that, where I went to Brigade HQ as a brigade major for two years. Then I was fortunate enough to be selected for promotion to lieutenant colonel: came back to England to the National Defence College for six months, did another six months at the MoD, and finally came to this battalion as its commanding officer in May of last year.

My career has gone far better, I think, than I'd any right to expect. You're very lucky to get the command of a battalion these days – but actually to get command of the battalion in which you've served all your time, and not only that but the battalion one's own father served his career in – well, naturally that gives me a tremendous sense of pride. I feel that I am undoubtedly carrying on a family tradition.

No quite correct it isn't entirely a matter of luck, no. There's a saying in the Army that if you get on it's one-third luck, one-third ability, and one-third knowing the right people. I've had my fair share of all those things, of that there can be no doubt. I'm now thirty-nine, and I have honestly achieved what I want at this point – my own battalion. I have another sixteen years to go, and what will happen in that time, well who can tell? But certainly so far it's been to me a thoroughly enjoyable life.

iii. *A not too bad life:*
Valerie Miller, corporal's wife

– I'm twenty-four going on twenty-five: I've two children one five and the other three, and I've been married to my husband for six years. We met when I was very young. I don't mean anything by it but I think perhaps I was a bit too young – Robby was the first boyfriend I'd ever had. We met in Northamptonshire, I was working in a shop in the town: he came in one day for some shoes and then right out of the blue he asked me if I'd go out with him. He didn't tell me he was a soldier on leave, did he? I would say we're on the whole very happy, we have our ups and downs but who doesn't? We've always been straight with each other, because I think that's the only way a marriage can be made to work. Right from the start before we was married he told me the old saying was true, if you marry a soldier you marry the Army. He said that would always have to come first, and although he was honest about it and although I said Yes I understood that and could cope with it, there've been times I must admit when I've felt I made a mistake.

Not in marrying Robby, I don't mean that because as far as I'm concerned he's the right man for me. I've wanted to have his children, and I've never looked at another man. But it's been much harder somehow than I ever thought it would. What I didn't understand was how difficult it would be with him being away so much. I knew there'd be times when he'd have to go away, but I thought of it in terms of me going with him. I wasn't used to such things as the six-month unaccompanied tour in Cyprus for instance – I thought me and the kids would be going with him on that. Also there's the matter of him having to go away such a lot on exercises: it's two weeks here, then home a week, then off somewhere else for ten days, and it goes on like that all the time. We once worked it out that in one particular twelve-month we'd had a total of only five months with each other, and that was including annual leave and all the rest of it.

There's not a lot you can do when you're left on your own at home with two young kids. Baby sitters cost a bomb, so about all you can do is sit and watch the telly. If you live here like I do on an Army estate, everyone round you's in the same boat: that's some comfort, at least you don't feel you're the only one in the world: but it doesn't stop it getting bloody boring. My parents live up in Liverpool, I can't drive and anyway we don't have a car, and train fares being what they are I only get up to see them about two times a year. Robby's parents are in Devon, at least his mother is: she's a widow, his father died some years back. Sometimes she comes up here to stay with me for a bit, but I wouldn't say we hit it off all that well, so there's not much joy there.

It gets on your nerves at times. You wonder where he is and what he's doing and whether he's all right. You can't even ring up if you get lonely, like you could if he was working in an office for instance. He rings me up when he's away, but that's always a matter of queuing up for a phone box, and it's expensive: about all he can do is ask how the kids are and that's about the extent of the conversation.

He's been in eight years now and he'll probably do twelve years or even twenty-two. That's something which he'll have to decide, and I shall leave it up to him. At least he's got the security of a job, which is a lot these days. And we know wherever we go we'll have a house, so there's a lot to be said on the bright side of it.

But the worst thing is as I say that it's a twenty-four-hour job. There's always the chance there'll be the knock on the door at night, telling him he's got to be off somewhere very early the next morning, or even sometimes he's got to go in there and then because he's wanted for something. A civilian person, if he wakes up in the morning and doesn't feel like it he can take a day off because he can ring up and say he's got a cold. But a man in the Army can't do that, he's got to go into camp to see the doctor and get properly signed off as sick. It's the Army that decides when he can have any day off at all: he belongs to them, he's an object they can move around and order about just as they wish. And that applies to me, his wife, I've got to go along with that.

Although like I say we've got a home wherever we are, it's never your own. You can't decorate it to your own choice: you can only paint the walls blue, lemon, pink, or light green, which are the regulation colours. You have to keep your garden just so all the time, and there's this feeling of being all your life under regulations. This is the side of being married to the Army that I was talking about that doesn't strike you when you first think about it.

Perhaps the other thing which is a bad part to it is the snobbiness. There's much more class distinction in the Army than anywhere else I know, and as far as the officers and men are concerned I sometimes get the idea the Army couldn't run without it. I'm not saying they're all the same because they're not: but there are some incredible people around, like officers who'll pass you in the street and look right past you even though they know perfectly well who you are. My husband last year was in one particular company where the officer in charge used to make a point of getting to know as much about the personal lives of his men as he could. His wife used to come round visiting his soldiers' wives, and she was a pleasant sort of woman – but of course a very la-di-da type, you couldn't really talk to her any more than she could talk to you, and so she can't have learned anything very much about anyone.

And it's not just the officers of course, there's snobbery among the different ranks too. A sergeant's wife for instance, she won't talk to a private's wife. It's a case of where the husband gets on, the wife thinks she has to put on airs and graces to keep up with what she considers to be his position. I suppose I'm being a bit unfair in talking like this, and although I keep telling myself that when Robby gets made up to sergeant it won't make any difference to me, I suppose it will. I suppose it will because in a way it has to: when you're a sergeant you go into the sergeants' mess and the wives go to social functions there, not to ones with the wives of other soldiers of lower ranks. This is what I was talking about earlier when I said I thought the Army couldn't run without its class system.

– When I was a girl? Heavens no, it never ever crossed my mind I was going to be a soldier's wife. I wasn't all that brilliant at school, but I think I probably thought I might be a secretary or a typist or something of that sort. I remember my mother wasn't all that keen on the idea of me marrying a soldier when I first took Robby home to meet her: but I think she's accepted it now. The last time I saw her we were talking about all the unemployment: she said I was one of the lucky ones who didn't have to worry about that subject. So I think she thinks it's got advantages to it now. Boredom and loneliness are the difficult parts of being an Army wife: plus also the fact that you have to put up with a lot of things which you don't get in any other walk of life, like the feeling somebody else owns your husband and has priority over him, rather than you and his children do. But I'd say on the whole it's a not too bad life.

3   Some of the Lads

i.   *Keeping your nose clean:*
     Chalky White, private

ii. *Hell and fucks:*
     Billy The Kid, private

iii. *Having thoughts:*
     Dongo Bell, private

iv. *Planning it all out:*
     Ginger Jim, private

i. Keeping your nose clean: Chalky White, private

— Michael John is what I'm really called, but I never get called it except when I'm at home, it's generally always Chalky all the time. Nearly everyone has nicknames, in fact some people I don't think anyone knows what their real names are.

Well, I couldn't say what got me in really, there'd been no one in the family in the Army. I think there was a recruiting officer came and gave a talk at our school and I liked the sound of it. They gave us some tests in the school if I remember it right I think, then if you passed those you were told you could go to the recruiting office if you wanted to. So I did that.

I wasn't very keen at school, I wasn't what you might call bright. I got one CSE in art that's all. My Dad worked on a farm in Norfolk but I didn't fancy that. He had to get up early every morning and go a long way on his bicycle. When I told him I was going to go in the Army he said I wouldn't last, I wouldn't stick it: I had a sister and another brother and they were both a bit dubious too. My brother said he'd never go in something where you got shouted at all day. Well, nobody shouts at him now: he's unemployed, he has been for a long time. Then I got a date not long after leaving school to go to Bassingbourne. We got picked up at the station by a bus: there was a whole lot of us and they took us and showed us round. We was all there for about one year I think it was. I didn't think it was hard, I liked it. I liked doing the weapon training, that was easy. I didn't enjoy the drilling, but you all muck in and have a moan about it afterwards all together. Anything you don't like, everyone has to do it anyway, cleaning out the rooms and that.

When I was old enough, I think it was seventeen and a half, I was still a junior soldier but they sent me to Berlin and I was there two years. As soon as I got to eighteen I signed on for three more years and then I signed on for another six after that. I've got another five to go out of that six. Germany was a fantastic place, the time I had there was really fantastic. (*Did you pick up any German?*) Yes I did, dozens of them, the girls were very keen on British soldiers, and if you wanted one you could have a different one every night. As a matter of fact I ended up marrying one. She was a schoolgirl that I met at a disco and she spoke very good English. We went out for a bit, and I went in for a bit if you follow my meaning, and then one day she said she was pregnant. Her Mum was all right about it, and her Gran who lived with them was all right too: but her Dad was a bit well let's say not too keen. When I came back from a leave in England once I gave him a plate I'd bought with a swastika on the bottom of it, and he didn't come to the wedding.

After I'd been in Germany a while I was going to be posted back here to England. I took her over the water on leave to have a look at it, and she said she thought she'd be all right. But she was only here a few months and she said she wanted to go back home on a visit. I had a feeling she wouldn't come back again and she didn't, so she's over in Germany now somewhere with the baby. It was probably signing on for another six years which did for it in her eyes. The baby's a little girl, she'll be about a year now: I don't know what she's called. We never talked it over about separating, we just both had the feeling it wasn't working and that was it. We had a quarter, a house, and I turned it in and went back into camp. You've got to do that if you're not married any more. I think the thing I missed most having to give up was the dog we had, it was a cocker spaniel.

To tell you the truth, I've never had such a good time in my life since I moved back in barracks with my mates. I've got a roof over my head, the food's not bad, I've got money in my pocket, I go out drinking in the town in the evening with some of the other lads, and there's always plenty of girls. It seems to me like the ideal way to live: so long as you don't do nothing foolish and make sure you're keeping your nose clean, always you'll be all right.

No, being a soldier, I wouldn't change it for the world, I'm really into the Army life. It might sound a bit corny but it's true, best of all I like being with my mates, and the only thing I don't like is getting up in the morning at five o'clock or whatever. And I don't like that you can't argue with someone above you, however big a cunt he is you've got to do what he says. I don't really want to get up very high in rank: I'd be quite happy to get to be lance corporal, and being corporal would be more than I'd hope for. The trouble is as soon as you do that you lose your mates because then they can't argue with you.

Yes, I'd have done exactly the same thing looking back, definitely, I mean about joining the Army. The only difference is I wouldn't have put that girl up the spout, or if I had I wouldn't have got married to her. I like it that I represent my country and the Queen, I'm very proud of that, I'm proud of being a symbol. I feel good about what I am, which is one of the Queen's soldiers. It means I'm somebody who's got somewhere.

ii.   Hell and fucks: Billy The Kid, private

— I went to Norwich Recruiting Office when I was sixteen and a half when I was working in a chicken factory. It was absolutely fucking terrible, I just felt I had to do something to get out. So I joined at seventeen. My mother wasn't very keen – well, I call her my mother but she's just someone my father lives with. I don't know where my real mother is, I think she fucked off when I was a very small kid. I've got two older brothers and I couldn't tell you exactly what they do, I don't come from what you'd call a close-knit family. My Dad does driving and things for a firm of wholesalers, but we've never been close. I wasn't all that bad at school: I got an 'O' level English and an 'O' level history plus 7 CSEs altogether. I wanted to be a PE teacher, but to go to college for that you had to have three 'O' levels. I wanted to do further education to get another one, but my father said it was time I started bringing some money in. He'd probably said the same to my two brothers: they didn't send any money home wherever it was they pissed off to, and I've not done either.

My mates gave me the name Billy The Kid, because they said I was a cowboy, I'm always riding the cows. So far I've been in four years, and I like parts of it and I don't like other parts of it. I keep thinking maybe I'll jack it in, but I want to get a bit of money behind me first.

To buy out I'd have to raise something like 700 quid, and I haven't
got that kind of money. Last time I went home I asked my Dad if
he'd lend it me but he wouldn't. He said I'd had a fair bit of money in
my time, and it was my own fault that I kept losing it. In fines and all
that shit, I worked out once I'd lost well over 3,000 quid in three
years. And on top of that done six lots in the cells of about
somewhere around eighteen weeks altogether. My main trouble
is drink. I suppose you could say I'm a typical bad reputation
squaddie. I get punchy, when I've got a few pints inside of me
someone only needs to look at me and I'll put one on them.

The other problem with me is that if I'm not drinking and
fighting, I'm drinking and driving: I've lost my licence three times,
and at the moment I'm on a two-year ban. There are times when I've
said I'm going to reform, but I've been good and I've been bad and
I've made no great progress either way. I enjoy the hell and fucks
more, so the way I look at it I might as well stay bad. I've met some
nice women around the world in places I've been – Germany,
Canada, Cyprus, Ireland, even Belize. Some of them there in Belize
were not too bad, so long as you weren't in a bright light: trouble
was, some of them were none too clean and you often picked up a
dose of this or that. One of the stupid things about the Army for me
is I'm always getting put on charges for fighting. My company
commander once said to me when I was up in front of him, "Look
Billy, you didn't come into the Army to be perpetually fighting you
know." I mean, what the fuck! You lose money for fighting when
you're in the Army: fucking fantastic isn't it?

I once thought things might be better if I didn't live in barracks, so
last year I got myself a flat in Cambridge: at the moment I'm living
there with a bird. I tell them here that I'm living with my brother. I
couldn't get an allowance for living out if I was just living with a
woman. I get nearly every weekend off, so we see a lot of each other,
and I go back there every night. She's been a good girl to me and I
hope we can stay together, maybe she'll help me settle down. She
wants a church and bells and all that stuff and us to be properly
married: I keep weighing it up, and maybe I'm getting a bit wiser,
but somehow I don't feel in the mood for marriage yet. I mean I'm
twenty-seven, and once you're married you've got to be a bit
responsible haven't you, you can't stay out whenever you feel like it
otherwise she gives you an earful when you come back. If they
didn't pay me such shit wages here I'd be more inclined to stay in,
but I don't like the ordering about and the doing all the stupid
things. Last week I spent all week dropping things on the ground out

of trucks, boxes we were unpacking. One of the sergeants started shouting at me so I told him I'd joined the Army to be a soldier, not a fucking box mover. He started threatening me with what he was going to do to me about it, and one of these days when something like that happens I'm going to hit an NCO or something and then that'll be it, they'll sling me out. I've been AWOL a few times, and once I took a pistol, so after a bit they start getting fed up with you.

I suppose the thing I like worst of all is the fucking officers, the second lieutenants and lieutenants: a lot of them are the fucking dregs, I can tell you. The one who's in charge of my platoon, he went straight out of school and went to Sandhurst, then he came along here at nineteen or twenty and he knows fuck all about anything. I'm not exaggerating, every time he goes to the toilet he can't decide whether to have a crap or a piss. Jesus.

And they do, a lot of them think they're some kind of fucking elite. God Almighty, I couldn't give two shits about that sort of person. But they're the sort of people who've the right to order people like me around. I think every officer should have to do two years as a private soldier and muck in with the rest of us. They shouldn't just be appointed to lord it over other people just because they come from posh homes and have decent educations. This is the worst thing about the Army, I hate that side of it. I know my language is bad and I behave as though I was an animal: but what I am is a soldier man, a fighting man, I'm the person all those ponces need because there'd be no Army without me. I don't want to be in fucking charge of nobody, but I do want a bit of respect for what I am.

I don't really know what the fuck else I want. If the Army can't cope with me, I don't know who could. If I got out I reckon it wouldn't be long before I was in big trouble outside. I feel like I'm just drifting along, but it's looking more and more to me that in another few years I'll be back on civvy street. Still, I keep hoping. What I hope most is that I'm going to meet this really wealthy bird, see, who's around forty and who likes a bit of rough. I have this dream that she goes mad about me and just wants me to screw her all day and all night. I'd be very happy doing my best along those lines. I don't really want to be a soldier and have to kill people, I'd sooner make some rich woman happy with my cock and live like that. Any woman who's in that position, and she wants someone like me and is prepared to pay for it and keep me in luxury, I hope if you hear of one you'll let me know. That'd be my idea of the ideal existence. I'd be what they call a mercenary you see: I really would, only in what I think's a nice sort of way, giving happiness and not causing harm to no one.

I'll tell you a joke to finish with. What's black and drops out of the sky? Bird shit and the Paras. Cheers.

iii. Having thoughts: Dongo Bell, private

– I do often have thoughts, I'm always having thoughts: the idea would be to try to get out. But I don't want to do that until it's the right time. I don't know when the right time would be, because things is very hard outside isn't they? Every time you read the papers or watch the TV, it's always about how the numbers of people who haven't got jobs is going up. I'd be very scared to go out of the Army, there's not a lot of jobs I could do and I think I'm better off where I am. I don't think being a soldier means very much, well not to me it doesn't: but I'd sooner be a soldier than be unemployed, that's for sure. I don't particularly want to get killed or anything like that, but I don't think there's much danger of that nowadays. The Falklands did make me think, because it would have been possible to get killed there, and when you read about things like that it does make you think. Some of my mates, they said at the Falklands time they hoped we was sent there, but I'm glad we wasn't. I've been in Northern Ireland a couple of times and I've heard shots being fired in anger, as they say. It was a long way away from where the barracks was, but it was near enough for me. My job then was barman in the officers' mess and that was near enough to anything for me. These are the sort of thoughts that you can't help having when you're a soldier and you can get quite worried about them. I'm all for the quiet life myself, and I think if they came along to me one day and said I'd got to go and fight someone I'd want to get out of the Army pretty quick before that happened if I could.

I've been in the Army ten years, I'm twenty-seven. I wasn't good

at anything at school, and my Dad was a civilian who worked with
the Army. I don't know much about it, he never talked about it
much, except he once told me it was a good steady job if you could
get in. And I have a brother who's in the Army as well, he's younger
than me. I've got two children, one four and a half and one who's
two. My wife and I have got a nice quarter and we've been seven
years married though I've been away for a lot of it. There's nothing
much I could say I like best about the Army except seeing a bit of the
world now and again I suppose, and getting money every month.
The thing I hate most is going away, and my wife hates that
especially as the kids are starting growing up. Our eldest, the boy,
he's just started school and she very often has complaints about him
from them. They say he's bad-mannered and hard to control and it's
very difficult for her. She wants me to go and have a talk with them
at the school. I don't think they properly understand the difficulties
you have when you're a soldier and have to keep going off.

The Army has done some good things for me. The most important is I've learned a lot of reading and writing. I was never very great
at that before I come in. I don't think there's too much discipline like
a lot of people do. Nowadays it's more people telling you things in
an asking way, but there's still some people don't like that. I reckon
I've got a good job now, but it's hard work. As well as the bar I have
to do waiting and washing up, and I push out a lot of hours. There's
times like last weekend when I start at ten of a Friday morning and
work all through until maybe Monday afternoon – that's Friday
night, Saturday night and Sunday night that I'm on duty for the
officers who are living in the mess. That messes up your own family
life quite a bit. You could get a bit bitter about it sometimes if you
were that sort of person. They're single men and they don't have
homes to go to for the weekend, while you're a married man and
you have to give up your weekend with your family to act as their
servant for them. Still, that's all part of the job isn't it?

The pay isn't all that good, a lot of people think it is but it isn't.
With the wife I go out for a meal in an evening about once every
other month because it's expensive even if you only go to eat at a
pub. You have to pay your rent, your gas and electricity and food.
We've got a little car, a second-hand one that we bought for a couple
of hundred quid: but that's an expensive item with the servicing and
the rest of it. We neither of us smoke, not the wife or me – but there's
the children's clothing and so on, and it doesn't give a lot to spare.
We don't go away on holidays to hotels or places like that. I've often
said I'd like to go and have someone wait on me for a change. When

I have leave, we usually go to her parents in Scarborough to give the kids a bit of seaside. I come from Northampton myself, but that's a town and we go and see my family sometimes only there's nothing much to do there except look round at the shops.

Mostly I go along with the idea that I'll do my twelve years and then leave. But it would be hard I think for someone like me to get a job, because there's not much I'm good at except something like working as a barman in a pub. If I did that, I don't think I'd get the wage to live like we do now because of the house and other things, and I think it'd be much more of a strain financially. I spend a lot of my time thinking about what would be the best for us, and I might even sign on again and stay in the Army.

This is the first time I've ever been interviewed by anybody. It's been OK as far as I'm concerned but it's hard to think of things I want to say. I'll probably think of things afterwards and if I do I'll write down notes about them so if we have another talk I can remember to mention them. I don't think I've said anything that I shouldn't have said, it's not as though I can give any official secrets away because I don't know any.

I'm called Dongo by my mates. It's a sort of nickname and I don't remember now how it came about. It's just one of those things that somebody calls you and it sticks. I think originally it had something to do with I used to bang my head with my fist like it was a bell when I was thinking thoughts about things.

iv. *Planning it all out: Ginger Jim, private*

— Eighteen I am, it was my birthday Wednesday. I did junior soldier for fifteen months and then I came to the battalion in January which was two months ago. I always wanted to join the Army, as soon as I came sixteen I went to the recruiting office in Lowestoft and they passed me. I don't have a Dad, I was brought up by my grandparents. My granddad had been in the Army on long service and he'd always said it was a good life and I suppose that's where I got the idea from. When I left school I'd no "O" levels or CSEs, and I wanted to get into the REME so that I'd have a bit of a training at something, but they said they'd no vacancies and all they could offer me was the Infantry so I took that instead. There was quite a few in my class at school who wanted the Army, and a lot tried but they didn't pass the exam which they sent you to Aldershot for. It was English, simple arithmetic, sequences, and general knowledge. It started simple and then it got harder as you went along. Like numbers: one, five, one, five, one – and then what comes next? The answer for that one's five. But then the next question would be one five one, five one five, two five one, five one six – and what would be the two numbers after that? Then they had intelligence tests, like you've got ten sparrows on a telegraph wire and you shoot one, how many will there be left? A lot of people say nine, but the answer's none because they'd all fly away.

After Aldershot I went to Bassingbourne Depot for fifteen months and that was good fun. They shout at you and run you around to see if they can make you feel like getting out. Specially if you try and give it to them that you're tough, then they'll give you a specially hard time. But if you act sensible or OK they'll treat you OK. I used to get home nearly every weekend. While I was there they said to me one day could I whistle, and when I said yes I could they said right, I was a drummer. I said what was that supposed to mean and they said I'd find out later. After a few weeks I did: it means you do all your ordinary infantry work, and then they learn you drumming on top. I do like it now I do: they teach you to read music, I enjoy it. You have side drums and flute players, and at the moment I'm hoping to go on to the flute after I've got up to the standard for drums. It's a bit special being a drummer. This is because you know your job and then you know another job on top as well. Anybody can learn to dig a trench and fire a rifle, but not everybody can play a drum. When you're on a march you're at the front, you're leading the parade, and that's an honour. You go on Freedom Marches, that's where the battalion parades through a town that it's got the freedom of, and we do travelling round shows – what they call KAPE tours, which stands for Keep the Army in the Public Eye.

When I think of all the things I've learnt since I started the Army, it's fantastic. As well as the drumming and music which I was saying about last time, there's map reading, all my weapons training and field craft, how to shoot straight, how to work with a machine gun, how to do marching properly. Sometimes it seems as though you can go on learning for ever. I've signed on for three years, but then I'll have the option of another three or another six years, whichever I choose. There's different grades of ordinary soldier from grade one to grade four. You take cadres, that's courses, for each grade, and then you take your lance corporal's, your corporal's, and so on as you go up. At the moment I'm planning it all out: I want to get to be a sergeant by the time I'm thirty or just gone, and then see how it looks from there.

Another thing it does for you is builds up your character and makes you a stronger-willed person. The Army makes you think quicker and react quicker and you grow up and look at life in a different way, you want to get on. When I went home last time my grandmother said to me that I wasn't her little boy any more. We used to have this thing that she would pick me up, but this time I picked her up and we had a good laugh about it and she said she was very proud of me.

The only place I've been to so far apart from England is Belize, where I went almost straight after Bassingbourne. That was my first posting, I was there on a six-month tour. They'd made it sound like Butlins when they was telling us about it at the depot, but Jesus Christ it wasn't exactly like paradise. I'll tell you more about it next time. You're going there yourself? Oh: well good luck then.

When I go back home and see my school mates who didn't get in the Army I feel like Rothschild to them in comparison. Most of them are on the dole, but I've always got money in my pocket. The last time I went home was on leave after we'd come back from Belize, I had £729 in my pocket. I spent every penny of it: I bought a lot of clothes and a stereo, and one night I took seven out for a meal in Lowestoft. There was my grandma and grandpa, a mate and his girlfriend, two mates I'd been at school with, and one of them's sister who was my girlfriend for the evening. We went to one of the big hotels and I told them they could have anything they wanted, as much as they liked to eat and drink. It was a great feeling: there's not many could do that at my age. Then when we got back to barracks after leave, all of us in the corps of drums had our own party with the money we hadn't spent when we were at home. We all put in all our money, and we had I think it was £1,100 which we gave to the NAAFI and asked them to give us a good evening. We put £350 of it behind the bar, everybody got roaring drunk and there was still some change. It was a very good night, we had a raffle for a portable telly and a digital clock radio. The adjutant came and the RSM dropped in for a bit, and it was a really good do.

So altogether from where I am now the future looks very good to me. I don't know what life is going to bring, but whatever it is I know I'm going to enjoy it because I'm happy. That's only up to now, and it can only get better as I go forward can't it?

4 And We in the Meantime

    i.   *Back home in somewhere:*
           Ingrid Wilson, private's wife

    ii.   *Racketing about: Jenny Donald,*
           lance corporal's wife

   iii. *One tries one's best:*
           Philippa Jordan, captain's wife

i. Back home in somewhere: Ingrid Wilson, private's wife

– I have been married with my husband three years now. I met him in Germany in a disco, we were introduced by a friend of mine who knew him, and we liked each other very much from the start so in due course we got married. This was in Celle where I come from, there are British soldiers there all the time, I think it is what is called a garrison town.

I have a younger sister who is called Marie. My mother works in an office in Celle with the British Army: my father is in a factory. I am twenty-five and in Germany I was a waitress. Well it is nice that you say so, I have spoken English since I was at school where it is a compulsory subject for all German children for the last four years of their education. Also, in Celle you meet many British people – not just the soldiers but their wives and their families if you work like I did in a café, and so you have a lot of practice to speak English. When Alan and me met each other, he was just coming to the end of his posting there. He was sent back to England at the beginning of May, and I did not like it without him so I came over here to England in June. I stayed with his parents in Suffolk, and I got to know them and they got to know me, also I was able to see Alan a lot and we still thought we loved each other very much and would want to get married. So we did that in August, and then the very first thing that happened after our honeymoon was that he had to go to Cyprus for six weeks and I could not go with him. He was only home for a few weeks after that when he heard the next thing, which was he was to go to Belize – that was for six months and is what is called an unaccompanied tour, that is that the wives and children cannot go. So off he went there.

In the first year of our marriage he had to go away on training courses too, so altogether we had I think it was only about fourteen weeks of our first fifty-two. That was a very good way to start our marriage, I think it made us like each other all that much more when the time was that we could be together. I have a little girl of eighteen months: no, I should say we have a little girl of eighteen months old, and her name is Anna Louise which is partly after Alan's sister and partly after my mother. Sometimes I have taken her over to Germany to see my parents: that is their photograph there on the bookcase, and they think she is very nice and they spoil her. I think she is definitely a little English girl with the way she looks, very like her Daddy.

Well, I have to say to you that I think I myself am now an English person. I made up my mind when I got married that if I was to marry a British soldier, then I would have to take his country as my own and learn how to become the same nationality as him. More and more it comes to me that this is my country here in England. The other day I was talking to a friend, the wife of another soldier, and I had said something to her that I had something "back home". She asked me where did I mean, did I mean here or did I mean in Germany. I said, "Oh I can't remember, I know it is back home in somewhere," and she laughed because she said it sounded as though I didn't know which was my home. But I think I do. It is here.

The most difficult thing for me is when he goes away, because although everyone is very friendly I do then miss having my parents. They are very good and write and ring me up or sometimes I ring them up, but this is expensive. Some little times I become lonely, but I am lucky with Anna Louise who is a real companion. For instance now while my husband is in Cyprus it is sometimes very lonely indeed, especially in the evening. But I read a lot of books – I like best J. B. Tolkein, and I am also fond of other English writers such as Paul Scott, *The Jewel in the Crown* I am reading just now because it was on the television and I thought it was very good. I think there are a lot of things written about England that are critical of the country, that have been written by English people and this is very good.

There are some German girls who have gone back after a while because they didn't like it. Next year we are going to Ireland, and some are already saying they do not like the idea of it and will go back to Germany instead. It is awkward to know what to do with a little baby, but the people I have talked to say it is not too bad, but there is very dangerous times. Of course just when you have made up your mind it is going to be OK, then there comes on the television some news of some shooting and you start to wonder again. But the Army looks after you very well, and I think you have to accept all the inconveniences – whether it is separation and your husband going away, or going to somewhere you do not very much like the sound of. That is part of being a soldier's wife.

Oh my goodness, what a very hard question! What character-istics do you have to have to be a soldier's wife? This is something that I do not know if my English is good enough for answering. I think the first thing is that you have to be prepared to take your share of the responsibility for the house. You have to take over the budgeting of the money, paying the bills and so on, because when your husband is away he does not want to wonder if he is going to come back to find a lot of bills and you have got yourself in debt. Also I think you have to be a practical person – you have to know how to mend things around the house, like electrical appliances and changing plugs and fuses and this sort of thing, or doing small repairs. Another thing you have to do – this is something I have only heard about from other wives, it has not occurred with us yet – is that if you have children you have to be ready when your husband comes back after he has been away, to step back a little and let him be the head of the household.

Inside yourself, I would say that the characteristic you have to have the most is equanimity. I mean by that you have to have the sort of temperament that you do not get down and depressed in your mind if you are alone. When your husband comes back, if he has been away on a hard exercise and living in trenches and holes in the ground in the pouring rain, he does not want to hear for the first thing what a terrible time you have been having – he wants to come to a warm and loving home, so you have to be able to put your own feelings in the background there. Another important thing is you always have to be optimistic and look on the bright side of things. I think you can only do this if you keep your mind occupied. I would say that I was not an independent person, that is not the word – but that I am capable of looking after myself. A lot of wives, when their husbands are away, they have to go always into someone else's house to drink coffee and have someone to talk to. But I like to be in my own house on my own. I would be glad to see a person, but I do not feel I have to be all the time running out. And well I think that is about the best I can do for you.

ii. Racketing about: Jenny Donald, lance corporal's wife

– This is my second marriage, this one's been so far for three years. I met George when he was on leave in Ipswich: I was working in a pub and he came in one night on his own. He looked very lonely, and I was sorry for him, and we got talking and he told me he was having to go off to Belize. I said I'd write to him if he'd like, and I did, and then a few months after he came back after his six months we went to the Registry Office.

I've got two children by my first marriage, a daughter Jackie and a boy Shaun, and now George and me've got one of our own a year old. It was difficult at first with the children, in fact my daughter took quite a long time to come round to him, but now everything's all right between them. At first she used to wet her bed, now she only does it now and again, and funnily enough only when he's not here. When he's here we have no trouble at all. The two eldest, they don't see their father ever, and we're putting in for adoption with them. We've had a bit of trouble at school, and the school's asked me to go and see them twice. Every time I do go up they ask me how the kids is getting on with their stepfather. I get really cross about it, that's all they seem to think about. We've never made a secret of it to them that he's not their father: he's very good with them and always says he hopes they'll look on him as if he was.

There's a big lot of security if you marry somebody in the Army: there is for me, and I hope there will be for my children. We had nearly five years on our own after my first husband went away, and it was very hard for me and for them. I can put up with George being away because it's different: I've got the security of his job and a house, and even when I haven't got him here I've got a proper home for the kids which is something I thought I would never see again ever.

But it's hard financially for a man with three children on a lance corporal's pay who's only been in for a few years. While he was a private, after the rent and lighting and heating and all the rest of it had been taken off, he only had £69 for the four of us to live on, which isn't a lot nowadays. Now it's still only a bit more, but we're happy, that's the main thing. It suits me, and when he's away on a course like he is now – he won't be back until Friday – all I do is go racketing about the house and waiting for him to come back. Look at it: the night before he comes, though, I'll have a big tidy up.

I don't really understand what he does: I think he's in anti-tanks and what they call Milans, they're some sort of gun but I don't know much about it. He doesn't talk about his work when he comes home, and if that's the way he wants it I'm not going to ask him questions. This course he's doing just now is part of one, I think they're called cadres or some word like that, which he's got to do if he wants to go up to corporal. It will mean a lot of hard work for him to get that far, but it'll make a difference with the money. At one time he said last year he was getting fed up and he was getting out because he didn't feel he was getting on fast enough, but I persuaded him to stop.

My parents had heard stories about soldiers, and they said the life wouldn't suit me. But I don't think they really knew what I went through the first time, because I didn't live anywhere near them. They didn't see me with the black eyes and bruises that my husband gave me. My George is nothing like that, thank God: he's a very quiet man, you often wouldn't know he was in the house. He has some of his mates come round here sometimes in an evening to have a game of cards and they're all the same, very nice and you never hear a swear word or anything of that sort. I sometimes say to him as a laugh that I think the Army must have a course for teaching men to be gentlemen, and he tells me they're all rough and tough and like animals. But I don't believe it, I think he's pulling my leg and he's very gentle when we make love and things like that. I told him once that if he ever left me I'd marry another soldier because I don't want any other sort of husband.

I suppose the thing I find the hardest – after George being away that is – is that your house isn't really your own and you've got to keep it immaculate. I'm not a very houseproud person and I'm not very tidy as you can see, with newspapers and plates and things all round everywhere. Most of all I think it should be a home for your children, and they're certainly not tidy, aren't mine. But if you get so much as a mark on the wall, you either have to redecorate the room yourself or it's taken out of your money when you leave. And you can't argue with them about it, if they say so that's it. Also I don't like it that the Families Officer will come round and have a look inside your house. He says he's called for a chat and to see if you've got any problems, but you can see him when he's sitting there looking all round at everything. I don't like the feeling of someone watching you all the time, and then when he goes he tells you something like that your garden could do with a bit of a tidy up. My next-door neighbour came in one day last week, she was effing and blinding because they were going to move and she'd spent two days cleaning the house from top to bottom to get it ready for leaving, and then they'd just told her she would have to pay £15 for not cutting the grass. Her husband's with the battalion that's going to Ireland and he's already gone on over there: she's got all the packing to do by the end of the month, and I think that's a bit hard.

About the only other thing I don't like much is that some of the wives, they can be really bitches. My husband's a sergeant, yours is only a lance corporal, that sort of thing. You have to bite your tongue sometimes because you know if you say something strong to her, her husband could take it out on yours. But there's not much, and I'm quite happy with the way things are now. I won't settle for it, I'm going to push him on to corporal because I think he's got it in him: I think he should get higher up than he is now, and I'm not just saying that for the money. He's a little bit younger than me, well three years to tell you the truth, and I think he lacks the confidence in himself. That first time I met him in the pub I remember then he was saying he had no confidence in himself and didn't think he really had the makings of a soldier. But I think he's done a marvellous job with my children, giving them a good home, and he never ever shouts at them or hits them or things of that sort. I think if there is bullies in the Army, and there is, then people like my George ought to get up into the higher positions where they have responsibility and where those above them can't bully those below them, or they can stop them if they tried to.

It's been a pleasure to have you come round for a chat, and any time you're near this part of the estate drop in for a cup of tea or a cup of coffee, so long as you don't mind the house being so untidy all the time eh?

iii.   One tries one's best:
Philippa Jordan, captain's wife

— I do honestly think that if you'd told me when I was seventeen that I was going to marry a soldier, I'd most probably have died of shock. I was a student at art college – very much into peace and flower power, Che Guevara posters on the wall of my bedroom, a pacifist and a socialist. If I ever thought about soldiers at all, I think I thought of them as thickheads who spent their days screaming orders at a lot of stupid men playing silly war games, and their spare time huntin', shootin' and fishin'.

I met Frank at a party in London, and I fell very heavily for him. I suppose the mere fact that he was at the sort of party I'd have gone to, where nearly everyone was like I was, must say something for him. He didn't seem out of place and we'd been sitting on the stairs and having a drink and talking for quite a long time before I cottoned on to what his job was. I remember saying to him "Excuse me, but do you mind telling me what exactly you do?", and him laughing and saying "I'm afraid you're not going to like this, I'm a soldier." I just said "Christ, I don't believe it," and we both started to laugh. Then after that, I remember I got frightfully upstage and polite. Until then we'd been arguing, or at least discussing: but as I say from then on I started saying things like "Yes actually you're probably right," and "Do you really think so?" and "Well every-one's entitled to their point of view." After a time he said to me "Please stop talking like that, I want to go to bed with you, I don't want to go on talking any more." I was sharing a flat at that time with two other girls from the college which was quite nearby, so we just left the party and went back there.

I suppose now at twenty-nine I have changed a lot, but I hope not completely. I feel life can't be quite as idealistic as one might like. I now see there's a lot of good in the Army, and a need for professional armed forces. To me the Army is a peace-keeping force and it's protecting people, making sure they have democratic freedoms, freedom of speech and so on. God, this sounds like the *Daily Mail* doesn't it? But I do really believe it, and I know Frank believes very passionately that that is what the Army is about. It was a big jump for me because I was very anti-Establishment minded, and I suppose one's got to say that you can't get much more Establishment than the Army. I hope I'm not being too much of a hypocrite if I say I find some of the other officers' wives awfully narrow in their outlook, and a lot of them are very snobby. But one mixes with the people one likes, and I'd like to think that Frank and I had our own coterie of fairly reasonable minded people. Yes they're all Army, of course one has to say that. I think that's because of the very nature of the job: you live in a very enclosed world of Army Army Army all the time – and of course we live here in an Army house. One tries one's best: not to get too incestuous or claustrophobic or whatever the right word is, not to talk about Army all the time and so on, but it's very very difficult not to.

I realize this most when Frank's away and I go with our two children to my parents in Lincolnshire, or to Frank's parents in London. Neither of them is an Army family and it's good for me to talk about other things. But that's about the only opportunity I get nowadays. But as you can see from all the different books we've got on the shelves round the walls, and our collection of records over there, our interests aren't entirely military. I'm something of an artist still myself, I hope: in so far as I can, I do try and get to art exhibitions and I love books of paintings like those big ones there. Frank is a bit of an amateur ornithologist, so all those on that shelf are bird books of one kind and another. I think it's very important too for the children not to grow up in a household where there's talk of nothing else but Army and Daddy's job. Our eldest boy Stephen is nine, and I wouldn't like him to grow up thinking he was necessarily going to follow his father into the Army. Our little girl Lucy, well she's only six so perhaps she'll have more of an independent life of her own: I sometimes think perhaps she could go in the art world and do design or something of that sort.

The reason I say I hope Stephen won't take it for granted he has to follow an Army career is that, to be perfectly honest, I'd like him to have a more settled way of life. It will in the end be up to him, but this is the side of it that I don't like, that we always have to move here and there and everywhere, wherever Frank's job takes him. So far he's been very fortunate and we've spent most of our time in this country. We were in Northern Ireland twice: once for two years, and we've been in Germany. But Frank has had quite a few jobs at Staff College, the MoD and so on, so we've been fortunate. And yes to be absolutely honest, I would prefer it if he were not in the Army. I miss him when he goes away, I think it's an unnatural life, and I'd sooner live some kind of ordinary existence where he could be with his family. But one has to set against that the knowledge that he's very happy indeed in his job, and that's most important. I wouldn't ever dream of trying to talk him into doing something else: but nevertheless if he came home one day and said he was going to leave the Army, I should be very happy. It's not just a residue of my feelings which I had when I was younger, but also because the security of the job which doubtless everybody will go on and on to you about is not necessarily of itself the be-all and end-all of life. Perhaps one should be more adventurous, and not live in such a cocoon as Army people do. I think you get into a frightful rut when everything is worked out so far in advance and there are no more surprises. For instance I know that at the end of this year we shall be going to Germany – and I suppose I'm still young enough to feel that although all this cut-and-dried business has a lot to be said for it, there's this curious sense too that life is going past. We in the meantime, the wives of the soldiers, we sit and watch it as though it was a film being shown outside our window.

Well I'm afraid that's all rather confused and I haven't expressed it very well. You must put it down to the fact I was mentioning earlier, that we're not really very used to talking to outsiders.

5 Voices of Experience

    i.   *An enormous amount of sense:*
           Adrian Allen, second lieutenant

    ii.   *All the worrying:*
           Peter Jones, captain

    iii.   *A killing machine:*
           John Taylor, major

i. An enormous amount of sense: Adrian Allen, second lieutenant

– I'm twenty-one in July, I've been in the Army for two years, and the whole thing is actually a bit of a mistake. What I mean by that is that my intention was to go into the Navy. My father is a serviceman and I was at boarding school, both prep boarding school and then after that on to another one: and I went in fact to a naval college, so how I ended up in the Army I don't quite know. From the college I had just about the right amount of qualifications to go to Sandhurst, and I think there was a bit of string pulling on my behalf, because I'm very glad to have got into the Infantry. I could very easily have gone as I say into the Navy as an officer cadet, and I think I wouldn't have enjoyed it at all. I can't imagine myself enjoying anything as much as I do the Army life. If I had to sum it up in one word, I'd say it was absolutely ideal.

In my very limited experience so far, I enjoy soldiering enormously. I enjoy the excitement and responsibility, and being an officer in charge of a platoon, which is thirty men. I can't think of any other job which would give me this amount of responsibility at my age. Millions of people I know think on a Sunday night "Tomorrow's Monday morning, back to work, oh shit." But I have got a job I love, I enjoy every moment of it, and so I regard myself as a very lucky man.

One curious thing about it is that I'm dyslexic. One of my jobs with my men is that they come to me to help me write letters for them, so I have to pass them on to my platoon sergeant. There's no way you can conceal that sort of thing: so we all make it into a huge joke. Actually it's a real pain in the neck, because although you can get round a lot of things by saying to somebody else "What does that say?", when it comes to taking exams and that sort of thing I have to have extra time for it. Or someone will be reading the paper and say "Christ, have a look at this," and it takes ages for me to make it out, and one doesn't necessarily want to have to explain to people why.

While I was at school I got two "O" levels, in geography and art, and failed all the others: then when I went on to college I got another four there, but they were mostly in subjects to do with nautical things. I'm not as you'll have gathered a great one for academics: I much prefer the outdoor life – climbing, canoeing, orienteering and so on, and those are the aspects of Army life which I enjoy most of all.

After I'd left college and been accepted for Sandhurst I bummed around for a while. I got involved with a firm who made boats, and worked for them delivering – I went to the Mediterranean, to Africa, and quite a few other places. At one stage I almost considered making boat-building my career, but it's dodgy and insecure and it had no kind of future prospects to it. Then I went on a number of courses and things including a spell at the depot at Bassingbourne. That's where they run you around and sergeant majors stick their faces about three inches in front of yours and scream at you, "You'll never make an officer, you fucking horrible little man, sir!" I thought it was tremendously good fun. One night I went to a party, and I don't know what it was but I felt full of confidence, I was on absolutely top form: the whole evening was brilliant, and then it was topped off for me when my mother rang up to tell me there'd been word that my final acceptance for Sandhurst had come through. I had to go on a special education course to polish up my exam results first, but of course by then I was well on my way and feeling that life was opening up spectacularly.

At Sandhurst they teach you determination. If you're going to be an officer, it's no use saying you can't hack something, you've got to get down to it and do it. I had a couple of terms there, then I visited the battalion, then on again for some more weeks of drill and final exams and interviews, and then came the passing out parade and ball. I'd no idea how I'd be accepted in the officers' mess as a twenty-year-old, but everyone was absolutely splendid and there were no hang-ups at all. So here I am, a very lucky man – in what I naturally consider to be the best battalion in the best regiment of the British Army, and there's nothing else I can say except that I think it really is, it's absolutely brilliant.

*   *   *

Being a soldier means to me that I'm doing a really worthwhile job. A few months ago when I was on leave I went to see my bank manager about getting a personal loan for a car, and I had to sit and wait for a while. I watched all the people working there, they all looked completely depressed and down in the mouth and as though they didn't know what life was about. Old men by the time they're thirty, you know the sort? And the women . . . The plainest lot of biddies you can imagine, not one decent looker among them. I tried to imagine myself spending my days among people like that, and I couldn't even start to think about it. They were doing nothing of importance, they were going nowhere, and they'd nothing to look forward to except boring boring boring days, one after another. But for me in my job everything is completely fresh and different all the time. We're going to Northern Ireland in a few weeks, I've managed to wangle myself on a couple of trips elsewhere, one to Canada and one to Norway, and now the whole world's my oyster. There are always exercises and courses, and there's bags of sport. I mean it really is a full and varied and worthwhile life.

What do I do for relaxation? Well that's not a very difficult question to answer, because I'm in the sort of job which is a relaxation in itself. I enjoy it so much that anything outside it is simply boring, and all I want to do is get back to doing what I'm trained to do. That is to lead my soldiers on their training – put on cam cream and cover ourselves with leaves and attack things, or dig trenches and live out in the open for days and nights on end. For instance we went on a brilliant exercise in Wales a few weeks ago. The pretence was that we'd been flown into somewhere, and it was an advance position and we had to wait for our supplies to catch up with us. We got there late in the afternoon after travelling all day in trucks and buses, and the first thing we had to do was dig in and make our position safe. We flogged ourselves to death doing that, then we got a message to say our supply trucks had been ambushed and we'd get nothing at all until the following day. We were all pretty hungry by then, but we had to make the best of it and go without.

The next morning we had to move to another position, and it had then got to midday and we still hadn't had a bite to eat. Then it started to rain, and we were all feeling pretty miserable and whacked out. But when you're in charge you have to give the lead, so even though I felt exactly the same way I couldn't let my men see it. I had to think about their morale, so I went around all the time chatting with them, cracking gags and that sort of thing. Not for one moment could I allow them to think my spirits were flagging. Finally at just past three in the afternoon when we'd had no food for more than twenty-four hours, the rations at last turned up. And what were they? A truck full of live chickens. So I had to sort out a couple of blokes to make up a slaughter party, and some others to pluck them. These were men who'd never done anything of that sort in their lives before, and there was a cooking and dishing up party to be arranged as well. We finally got to eat at about six o'clock in the evening in the pouring rain under the trees, and believe me those chickens tasted marvellous. I thought the whole thing was brilliant, whoever'd thought it up really knew what he was doing. And you see once you've gone through that sort of experience, you've progressed – you know you can cope with that sort of situation, and you're that much more mature than you were before. When you think about it, it all makes an enormous amount of sense.

Marriage? Well that's something I suppose I shall think about one day, but I'm enjoying life too much to waste time at present in looking for girls. I don't really want any kind of social life, I'd rather be training in Wales than drinking with some silly Henrietta at a party. We had a Ladies Guest Night in the mess last month, and someone said he'd provide me with a girl who was the sister of his girlfriend. I put on my best bub and ticker or whatever it's called, but I think he was actually playing a dirty trick on me, because when she turned up I can tell you she wasn't exactly Bo Derek. All the other officers were letting me see they were laughing behind their hands, and I felt a right idiot having been stuck with this creature for the whole evening.

ii. All the worrying: Peter Jones, captain

– When you ask that question, the answer is that in many respects I've been in the Army all my life, since my father was a professional soldier and was in this particular battalion. I've actually been in it myself for fifteen years. And I think too that I've always known I would join the Army. There was never any direct pressure, just the home environment: I never really gave serious consideration to any other profession. I can say, and do without being in any way critical of the procedure, that it was almost a formality.

When I was ten I went to a prep school, a boarding school for officers' sons. That was something I particularly enjoyed, even though I was not specially good academically. I hadn't much in common with boys of my own age because I was more travelled than they were and tended to mix with the older ones: but I was very gregarious, and got on well with people. I was supposed to go on from there to one of the posher public schools but I failed the entrance exam. Looking back, I think that was one of the best things that ever happened to me, because I went to another school where I had a marvellous time and again thoroughly enjoyed myself. The place was fairly small, I went at the age of thirteen and stayed until I was eighteen. I collected a few "O" levels, I think about five altogether which was sufficient for me to go to an officer cadet school: but my father refused to let that happen, he said I was to do "A" levels in order to get to Sandhurst. I was very unwilling about it and ploughed the exams, which put the kybosh on things. As a result of that, after the summer holidays I joined this regiment as a private on what is called a "special" type of engagement, which allows people such as myself to get out if one doesn't make the grade, rather than stay on in the ranks. I went to the depot, then to an Army school to do a course where everyone else was like me, I mean needing brushing up educationally. I passed the required standard and I was granted a place at Sandhurst, where I went for two years and thoroughly enjoyed it. When I passed out I was then commissioned into this regiment and in fact this battalion, as a second lieutenant. I keep repeating that I've thoroughly enjoyed things, and I think as a young person I did, without a shadow of doubt. I had a rather rigid and disciplined life, and that appealed because it was how I'd been brought up for as long as I could remember.

The beginning of my Army career was splendidly fortunate. I was sent off to a whole series of places one after another – Gibraltar, Kenya, Cyprus, Malaya, to name only a few. I thoroughly enjoyed it all and it was a marvellous beginning for a young officer. With periods in this country in between I did a couple of tours of Northern Ireland, and then spent the best part of three years in Germany. Then I went to Staff College, and eventually became an instructor for two years as a captain: I was teaching anti-tank weapons and tactics. We went on exercises to let me see, Cyprus and Denmark are the principal places I remember. Then there was another period in Northern Ireland, which I found quite exciting: there was a period of great trouble, a lot of shooting, and we took several casualties. Another period at Staff College, and now here I am.

I'm a professional soldier, an infanteer, and in a way I suppose I could be called a typical soldier. But I don't think it's fair to categorize people in that way, particularly officers who are all very different characters. I have my own views, I am an individual: and within the setting in which I follow my profession, I am encouraged to be an individualist – i.e. someone who thinks for himself and doesn't just live slavishly by the book. One is only typical in belonging to what might be regarded as a large, indeed a very large and extended family. This is my environment as it is that of others. When you come back from leave and your sergeant says to you, "Jolly nice to see you again sir," and he really means it – well, that's one of the great rewards of the life, because you feel the men under you have not only respect but also affection for you.

I'm married, yes, and I have my own family: but it's nice to feel that my family is part of a larger one, and if anything were to happen to me that they would be looked after. As soldiers we do all make an important and positive contribution to society even though society doesn't always recognize it. But we're ready for every crisis and emergency in whatever part of the world we're called upon to go to. We act only defensively, which is not something every soldier in every army in the world can say. Most certainly yes I regard the Falklands business as a defensive action: I don't see how anyone could say it was anything other than our government reacting in a perfectly legitimate way to aggression performed against British subjects. Admittedly we had to be aggressive to throw our country's enemies out, but that's exactly how we're taught and trained to use aggression, in a defensive capacity way. We won, we gave an example to other people as to what would happen if they tried the same thing, and I think we can be proud of the way we acquitted ourselves. Though I didn't serve there myself, nor did this battalion, we were more than ready and willing to go, down to the very last man. It'd be true to say I think I could claim every soldier who didn't go to the Falklands felt a sense of disappointment at not being given the opportunity to show what he was made of. So if that's what's meant by being "a typical soldier", then I think it's a claim I and everyone else would be proud to make, and would be proud to have people say about us.

We've recently as you know been carrying out a ceremonial parade on the day of a royal visit. You'll hear different points of view about this sort of activity, but as someone who was closely involved with putting on what I think could fairly be called an immaculate parade, I can say without hesitation that it was a very proud day. I don't agree at all with those who say this sort of thing has little or no relevance in the modern army, the trooping of the colour, the drilling display and so on. It's all part of a very long and important tradition, and instils in everyone who takes part in it a sense of pride in who they are and where they belong. This is the battalion doing something which it does very well: being smart, functioning as one, and upholding the primary virtues of neatness and smartness under the scrutiny of a royal visitor.

Drilling you see is designed to teach soldiers to obey orders instinctively and to act as one. Soldiers are much more intelligent today than they used to be: they have to be, because their weapons and equipment are pretty technical pieces of kit. But come the hour and come the day, they still need to have had instilled into them an instinctive obedience to orders. You cannot have debates on a battlefield, you cannot have doubts and hesitations: the soldiers must trust their leaders and do what their leaders say without so much as a second thought, and they will only do that if their leaders have shown that they are capable of giving them an example.

As one such leader, I have to confess I spend a large part of my waking life worrying – all the worrying that I am going to get things absolutely right, whether they be exercises or parades. It's essential for my men that I should, because the day could well come that the balloon went up and we would have very little time to deploy our forces and make our decisions. Those in the higher echelons of command, right down to the lower ones: all have this tremendous responsibility. Of course it's not something you allow to get you down, you're trained to carry it. But effectiveness only comes through constant awareness of human fallibility, your own and other people's. That's an example of what I mean by worrying.

iii. *A killing machine: John Taylor, major*

– I look upon being a soldier as . . . may I pause for a few moments please before I answer this? Yes, I look upon being a soldier as being a member of a disciplined organization which may and indeed must, if necessary in the final analysis, use a considerable degree of force when ordered to do so to protect the country's interests. While we are fortunately more at peace than at war, the whole purpose of our profession is to prepare ourselves to go to war if that is what we are required to do in the interests of the country. That includes activities which are not necessarily forceful, in the sense of using force in support of the civil power as one of its mechanisms for the maintenance of law and order. In the first type of action which I was speaking of, it directly means to me as an infantry soldier the act of killing people. Or perhaps I should say causing people to be killed, because that then includes both sides of the activity – to be prepared to go into a situation where people will be killed as a result of one's actions, and where oneself and one's colleagues may be in turn be killed. I do not take any pleasure in it, but it is at the very core of the need for our existence.

I am a Christian and I believe it is wrong to take life. I think it has to be accepted though that there are certain situations where this is the only solution that can be adopted. Either you fight or you do not: and it would be a nonsense to fight without the intention of winning, and an even greater nonsense to put restrictions on what one was prepared to do to win. I think the issue cannot be avoided, and it is the first thing every infantry soldier has to resolve, this issue as to whether he could kill or not. If he can't there is no point in his being a soldier.

One's whole knowledge of society, of history, and of human nature, shows there is a requirement for a properly organized and trained armed force. Most importantly of all, it should be properly controlled and used only minimally: I do not agree, nor fortunately does any other responsible person in this country, that the Army should be a law unto itself. It is a servant of the government, an arm of policy – but it should have no say in policy making.

If you don't mind I would prefer to say as little as possible about my background and career, as I have no wish to be at all identifiable. Indeed if I thought there was danger of that, it would obviously affect both what I said and how I said it, and I'd prefer to feel free to express my views without anyone being able to pinpoint who I was. So as far as my background is concerned, I'll say only that I've been in the Army quite a number of years, and that I joined it from university instead of doing a PhD. My family has no connection in the past with the Army. When I was at university and decided to become a professional soldier it seemed to me a logical progress. It was necessary for me to find a profession which was intellectually fulfilling and neither commerce nor education seemed to offer the future sort of opportunity I wanted. I wanted a structured life, and to be doing something I considered to be important to society. Yes that's true: it sounds almost like a job description of the priesthood, so possibly that's why I chose the Army rather than the Church. I take life quite seriously, I'm possibly a bit of a loner, I'm rather more intense than many people I know, and I think I'm a thinking man but also a man of action. I like outdoor activities, I like the responsibility of being an officer and a platoon commander, and I enjoy soldiering. Having said that I should point out that I prefer function to form – in other words I don't care very much for parade ground soldiering.

I don't enjoy what are called Freedom Marches, where we parade through towns. They don't often occur, but to my mind they're largely a waste of time because we have much more important and valuable training which we should be concentrating upon. It's somewhat ironic that they're expected of us by some members of the public: civic dignitaries in particular always enjoy hobnobbing with the Army, and they like to have a parade in their town. One has to say after all that we are in the final analysis society's Army, so I suppose we have the responsibility towards them to let them look at us in our fancy dress and hear us with our band once in a while. There's a phrase: if I remember it correctly, where we have the freedom of a town this gives us the right to march through it with drums beating, flags flying, and bayonets fixed, or it may be swords bared or some other such phrase. It shows you how much attention I pay to it that I can't remember the proper words.

But I regard all that as an anachronism. If the public wants to see its Army it should see its modern Army, not one part of it indulging in some kind of pantomime. The Army is after all a killing machine. It seems to me in a sense society is trying to pretend to itself that it isn't, when it watches it on parade. I think there is a lot of woolly thinking about this aspect of the military. A soldier is a soldier is a soldier, and is not a toy to be used for public entertainments.

But no, I don't regard individual soldiers as no more than individual killing machines, nor do I think they should be trained to be so. They are human beings and they should be trained to think and act as though they are, not as though they're feelingless hooligans. I think you do get a situation with some armies, particularly in certain countries in South America where I've been, where the military are an extension of the not very pleasant personality of the ruler of that country. Our Army, I think I could safely say, in everything it does has a care and a concern – not only for its own members but for those it is opposing. I don't believe that British soldiers ever get out of hand: they are very strictly trained to obey orders, to take a great deal of provocation but not to react individually, only on command and under command. I think this is something we can be proud of, and it would be quite horrifying if any other situation obtained. I don't want to give the impression either that I'm unusual in thinking like this: all the senior officers I know feel exactly the same way, that they carry a responsibility to the whole of society, not just to the governing part of it.

I regard soldiering as intellectually fulfilling. It makes constantly changing demands on one's abilities both physical and mental, and it brings its quiet rewards in the sense of feeling that one is achieving something necessary and indeed important. It's a profession which I think anyone can and should take great pride in. I don't believe soldiers are an elite, or are better or worse than other members of society, though of course I like to think as anyone would that one's own contribution is important. I would be perfectly happy never to have seen active service of any kind. I don't glory in what fighting I've done, but nor on the other hand am I waiting impatiently for battle. If it's necessary, and when it's necessary, I will go where I am ordered to go and do what I am ordered to do. Yet at the same time I would dispute this made me in any sense an automaton. I am what I am by choice: if it no longer satisfied me to be like this I would leave the Army tomorrow. A time of dissatisfaction? Well, the one that immediately springs to mind is Northern Ireland . . . but I'll leave that for another occasion.

6 Forwards, Sideways, Backwards

i.   *Keeping up with going up:*
     Mary York, sergeant's wife

ii. *Finding time to be me:*
     Julia Clark, lieutenant's wife

iii. *Right in the shit:*
     Audrey Brown, private's wife

i. Keeping up with going up:
Mary York, sergeant's wife

– My husband is a sergeant and we've been married for almost exactly eight years. We met in Cyprus: I was at school there, my father being in the RAF at the British base, and he – my husband, I mean – he was an Army lance corporal. I'd say I was normally bright at the servicemen's children's school: not in any way special. When I left I had two "O" levels and six CSEs. My best subject was maths, and I was aiming at a career in a bank. I came to London to work in one for a while, then I had a little time with a firm of accountants: and by then I'd made up my mind, as Colin had, that we were going to get married. I gave up ideas of a career of my own at that point when I was aged twenty: it's not possible if your husband is in the Army, because you know you'll be constantly moving around.

I was fortunate in that my husband was soon posted back to England: we hadn't intended getting married quite so soon, but we thought we might as well take the opportunity. We now have a little boy, and in due course we'll increase our family. I'm not sure yet exactly when, but we'll work it out so it fits in with my husband's moves. Perhaps if we go to Germany that would be the right time, after we've been settled there for a while. I'm very used to service life: I can't really imagine any other kind because of my father. I seem to get itchy feet every two years or so and I enjoy the moving. We've been to Northern Ireland: I enjoyed it there, I thought it was a very beautiful country. The longest we've been separated was when Colin was in Belize for six months last year. Our little boy, whose name is Justin by the way, is five: he's a very nice polite well-behaved little boy, and he goes to a nursery school in the mornings which he likes. At twelve o'clock I shall go and fetch him in the car.

More coffee? I was talking about Belize and it being our longest separation, wasn't I, yes. I found it lonely of course, but I had Justin: and I constantly reminded myself that poor Colin didn't. I tried to send him letters and photographs and tapes two or three times a week, telling him every little trivial thing that Justin had been doing or saying, so that he wouldn't feel too isolated. When it got to the half-way point of his stay out there, I made myself a little meal with half a bottle of wine one evening, to celebrate from then onwards it would be downhill all the way as they say.

I can cope perfectly well on my own. My parents live up in the north so I don't see a lot of them: but I'm not the sort of person who worries at being alone. To tell you the truth, although I wouldn't choose it, I quite like being independent and self-sufficient. It also makes for a constantly changing relationship when your husband is away, at home, away again and so on. I like that. I can though foresee a problem coming with Justin though, because he's beginning to be aware of the meaning of time, and is starting to ask questions like "When will Daddy be home?" Even more difficult we find is that when Colin is here, he asks him "How long will it be before you go away?" We show him the number of days on the calendar, and we try to make a game of it, a counting game. But I'm not entirely sure this is a good thing. You do have constant problems of adjustment to and with a small child. Justin for instance is used to asking me to do things for him rather than his Daddy, because I'm the one who's here all the time. If he wants to take the lid off a tin and can't manage it he'll bring it to me in the kitchen, even though Colin's sitting there. To get him used to the idea that Colin'll also do things, I try to remember to send him back to him and ask him to do it. It's not easy. There's inevitably a close bond between us, and I think it's important that Colin shouldn't be shut out, or feel that he's being shut out: but at the same time I have to give Justin the impression that I can manage – as indeed I can – without Colin being here when he's away.

Colin's always had a very clear idea of where he was going, in the Army I mean. His goal is of course to become the RSM. The Army is his life, he's proud of the progress he's made, and if you've devoted your life as he has to something obviously you want to get on as far as you can. Although it's too soon to talk about it, I know if he was given the opportunity he'd go on to take a commission. My father was an officer, so this wouldn't prevent us from making the necessary social adjustments. But at this stage I think we just try and keep our sights on RSM. I do actually rather fancy myself as the RSM's wife. That's a little bit of snobbery perhaps. But it's a big job for a woman, you're right at the heart of things if you do it conscientiously, and I'm quite sure I could do it. So far I feel I've done very well at keeping up with going up: by this I mean at the social functions, first of all in the corporals' mess and now in the sergeants' mess.

All my friends around here on the estate are married to soldiers, and in quite a number of cases I haven't the faintest idea what rank their husbands are: I don't know whether they're below, equal with, or above Colin, and I'd like to keep it like that. I can't stand these wives who'll only talk to other wives whose husbands are on the same level as theirs. But I think one should be honest about it: there are some women I know who won't have anything to do with the wife of someone who's of higher rank. One particular lady who lives only a few doors away from here, we stopped outside for a chat one day and I asked her if she'd like to come in one morning for a cup of coffee. Do you know what her reply was? You wouldn't believe it I'm sure, any more than I did when she said it. She said she'd like to, but her husband had told her not to get too chatty with me because my husband was his platoon sergeant and he felt I might be spying on his domestic circumstances. He'd told her something like "The job's the job, and we don't want our private lives being brought into it." I think it's incredible, but there you are.

I think that kind of attitude must make both husband and wife unhappy in the Army, because it is a world of its own and you do have to be of a certain type to fit in. You have to understand its workings and its very complicated structure on both the social and the family side. Perhaps I'm very lucky in never having lived at all in civvy street, so I have a natural understanding which I feel makes me fit in well. I don't think I really know the meaning of that word "institutionalized", but if by it you mean do I lead a very ordered existence obeying the rules, formal or informal, said or unsaid, laid down by other people, and conforming in every way – well then the answer is unhesitatingly "Yes". I absolutely have that kind of existence: it's the only one that I like, and I wouldn't want to change it for anything.

ii. Finding time to be me:
Julia Clark, lieutenant's wife

– When you marry a soldier, you go back into society about a
hundred years because you become a camp follower. The act of
marriage is making a choice – whether you're going to lead your
own life, or whether your life as a person is going to be entirely
secondary. If that's the choice you make, then you get the most out
of it that you can: but you're no longer a free individual, your life
follows lines that other people have drawn. There are perimeters or
what's the modern word, parameters – limits beyond which you
can't go. I'm not intending to sound bitter or disillusioned about
this. I'm not: I made my choice, which was to marry Brian, and if I
could go back to that time eleven years ago knowing all that I know
now I'd make the same choice again. I love him, he loves me, and we
are very happy together with our three children. This doesn't mean
though that I have to pretend our life doesn't have difficulties. It
does, everyone's does. It's not been one long glorious honeymoon,
nor did either of us expect it ever would. But we have the great
advantages of security of career, and an interesting life in that we
move from one place to another, and see different countries and
different parts of this country. Brian's prospects look good, people
tell me he's good at his job: and people of higher rank than he is
also say he's something of what's called a "flyer". Comparatively
he's young for the rank he's got to: he's really an acting captain
now.

We have a very busy life, but I like to think it doesn't stop me entirely
from finding time to be me. By that I mean that despite what I said to
you the other evening about being an Army wife, I do feel I've
protected myself from totally abandoning my own personality. For

instance Brian and I co-operate and have discussions about the children, about their education, about everything to do with us as a family. We both share the same sense of humour, laugh at the same kind of things, find more or less the same people either likeable or unlikeable. But we also have fairly well defined differences too. I regard myself as some kind of vague Christian, or that I'm at least basically someone with religious belief. Brian isn't: he's what you might call a devout agnostic, and we sometimes have quite serious differences between us in our outlook on life. We're also rather apart politically: he's always telling me that I'm a High Tory and that I don't have a clue what life is about. I don't think he'd claim to be a socialist, but he's certainly SDP and our political discussions sometimes get quite acrimonious.

I wouldn't myself think that I was a dreadfully reactionary Tory. My father is a farmer, and in recent years he's become what I suppose might be called a wealthy landowner. I can't help my background, but I hope I'm not strongly class-conscious or any nonsense of that kind. Brian comes from what he proudly proclaims to be a working-class family, by which he means his father was a station-master. He must have been academically very bright I think, because he went to a state school and then a grammar school for a couple of years, and from there he won a scholarship to Manchester University. He's a lot cleverer than I am intellectually, I accept that. But then girls like me from moneyed families sometimes don't get decent educations: they're sent to schools where the most important thing is that they should be "nice". Damn the academic standards or the mental stimulation, she's only a girl and as long as she makes a good marriage who cares? My parents weren't alone in having that kind of attitude about their daughters, and both my sisters and me had what I now see was a poor education because of it.

This must all sound like a dreary catalogue of complaint about my life, but the main thing to me is it's an account of something which is now very firmly in the past. I met Brian when I went to an extremely silly party where there were a lot of extremely silly people – I think it was the twenty-first birthday party of one of my friends in the shires. The only person there as far as I was concerned was this very truculent young university student, who made it very plain he disapproved of nearly all the guests: just by his expression when anybody brayed or laughed, which is what a lot of them did nothing else but. He was the boyfriend of another girl there, so I suppose I did the rather dreadful thing of pinching him. But I don't regret it, and he's told me since that he very much fancied me from the first moment he set eyes on me. Now I'm sounding rather toffee-nosed and a bitch into the bargain, aren't I?

Where was I, yes, about our meeting and Brian being at university. To give you an idea about how dotty I was about him, I went and got a job and a flat near Manchester so we could be together, and we went on from there. He kept telling me that at the end of his university period he was lined up for an Army commission, and we seriously discussed whether he should go ahead with it. I thought that I'd take to the life, and anyway I didn't want someone to give up his chosen career just for me. I was quite prepared to go on living with him without us marrying, but it was Brian who was insisting that he wanted to make our partnership a formal one.

Within a very short time of our marriage, which was just after he'd gone into the Army and been posted to this battalion, I really came down to earth with a bang. He was sent on a four months' tour of Northern Ireland, and I found myself alone in a quarter, a rather shabby semi-detached house in a garrison town. I didn't know anyone and no one knew me. I absolutely hated it, particularly as it was at a time when things in Belfast were very serious and the news every day was of street fighting and riots. I thought the only thing to do was get a job to keep my mind occupied. But what can an expensively brought up young lady do for a job in a garrison town? I literally had no skills of any kind: even if I could have got some sort of secretarial job I wouldn't have been able to keep it because I couldn't even spell properly. I tried one or two of the shops to see if they wanted an assistant but none of them did: and then by a stroke of very good luck – because I had toothache actually – I went into a dentist's and found they were looking for a receptionist because the one they had was leaving to have a baby. So I came out minus a tooth but with a job, and that did help for a while.

After about a year and a half I think it was, we went to Germany. That was when the pleasant and happy part of Army life really began. We had a quarter which was a rented house in a small town about twenty miles away from where Brian was based, so we weren't surrounded by no one but Army people. We both learned German, and made our own circle of friends – some of them local people, some of them other officers and their wives. It was a very happy period indeed, and there we had our second child. Brian had been on an exercise and we expected him to be back for the birth, but Lydia decided to arrive early, so I was on my own. Our elder son was looked after by some kind German people until Brian came home about five days afterwards.

I wonder what similarities, if any, you're finding between Army wives when you talk to them? I hope you won't find us all an entirely dreary lot who feel all we are is merely pawns. But I suspect to an outsider almost inevitably that's how it will appear. "Camp followers" was the expression I used when we first talked, wasn't it? I'm afraid basically that's exactly what we are though . . .

iii.   Right in the shit:
Audrey Brown, private's wife

— Forwards sideways backwards: I don't know whether I'm coming or going and I haven't for over a month now. I don't know where I am except right in the shit, that's for sure. He's gone back into barracks and I'm due out of here a week Monday. And there's the two kids to be thought of, so I'll probably try and go back to my Mum's. But I'm not keen and she's not keen, and it means taking Barry away from his school again. The poor little sod's had seven different schools already and he's still only nine. Still that's the way it is with the Army: once your marriage's broken up, as far as they're concerned they don't give a fuck for you any more, you're on your own. I went down the Families Office and asked them to help, and they turned round and said, "Well you're not our responsibility any longer, you'll have to work things out for yourself." Fucking charming, that shows you what you're worth in their eyes. I should think the best'd be to go home to Belfast, because I don't know anywhere else to go and that's a fact. Twenty-four, and my life finished, that's as it looks to me: two kids and a hard time, that's all I've had out of it so far, a real fucking disaster.

Those who tell you it's a good life, they must have found things I never did. I was stupid from the start. They say the Irish are ignorant and stupid don't they, well I must be a prime example. I was only eighteen when I fell pregnant by Benny, and he give me all these tales

about what a different life we could have together in England. What
he didn't mention was that he'd have all the good times, and I'd be
stuck here over this side of the water with the kids while he was off
enjoying himself. I don't think they make that plain enough to you.
When he was last year in Belize he was all the time sending me
photos and tapes of himself and his mates enjoying themselves,
that's all.

They even went to fucking Mexico for their leave, didn't they?
There was plenty of women and drink and sunshine and all the rest
of it there: here it was in the middle of November, I felt really pissed
off about it I can tell you. I don't want to give you a long list of
moans about what a good time they have when they're away, but he
never made no secret of it there were plenty of girls for the soldiers,
and that's God's truth. He boasted about it, he used to think it was
funny. But on the Army houses estate here, if a wife so much as says
"Good morning" to the milkman, there'll be some kind person
who'll write and tell her husband about it and he'll pass it on to
yours. You know, I think Army wives are the worst gossips in the
world.

If you ask me to try and sum up Army life, as an Army wife talking to
an outsider, well obviously because of my situation I'm going to give
you a biased account aren't I? But I think the first thing people don't
understand is that when you're married to a soldier you're still a
civilian: so you don't necessarily accept the rules and regulations
even if he does himself. In civvy street for example you can say to
your husband you'd sooner he didn't do this, that or the other: but
in the Army you can't, because all the time for twenty-four hours
out of every twenty-four he belongs to them and not to you. I
thought the life would suit me but it didn't and it never has done. I
married him as a person, I didn't intend to marry the Army. But I
sometimes wonder if there's any real people in the Army, ordinary
people, people like us. If I look back on it now and try and think
about it calmly, I must say perhaps in some ways I considered it as a
way out for me from the life I was leading of a Belfast shop girl. I
knew I was a strong-minded person, and I thought I'd be able to
make more out of life with him, but I've found out I couldn't.

The loneliness which everyone tells you is something everyone
suffers when their husband goes away, and there are lots of other
jobs where that's part of it – well, you can survive those times
because the rewards outweigh the disadvantages. But the kind of
loneliness which I've found the hardest is that the Army is a

completely old-fashioned male society. Even when he was here at this barracks, everyone thinks it's perfectly OK for them all to go out together in the evenings drinking in the pub and leaving their wives at home to look after the kids. Or he'd bring some of his mates round here in an evening for a game of cards, and they was sitting at the table there and drinking beer till one or two in the morning. You know, an occasional word to me like "Any chance of some tea, Aude?" Or maybe that was just him, I don't know.

And another thing is you don't feel you're a real person at all, you feel you're more part of your husband's equipment or issue. That's a very bitter thing to say, but I've been on the receiving end of it so much and for so long that I really do feel it. I found that feeling almost much more difficult than anything else at all, in as far as being the wife of a private soldier was concerned. And living on a huge estate where everyone else is Army, well I'm just not cut out for it. In civvy street it couldn't happen that if your husband had left you with two children to look after, then as well you'd find yourself with no place of your own to live. All my friends, or at least my acquaintances because I don't really have any friends, they're all the wives of soldiers. So so long as they stay like that, then they'll be looked after and granted security. I know people whose marriages aren't so good, but they stay living in the same house because the husband doesn't want to make things more difficult for the wife than they are. But that wasn't how it was as far as Benny was concerned: he told me to my face he'd prefer living in barracks with his mates, and so off he went.

I shall be glad to get away from here. I do I feel I stick out like a sore thumb.

7 No Problem

i. *The tallest man in town:*
    Geoff Marshall, private

ii. *Going out of my way:*
    Joseph Smith, corporal

iii. *Wait till you see me chick:*
    Jack Green, sergeant

iv. *Having a quiet laugh:*
    Roger Dawson, staff sergeant

i. The tallest man in town: Geoff Marshall, private

– No problem no, no problem about being black, not in the British Army. It doesn't make a scrap of difference to anybody. OK the sergeant shouts at you "Come on you lazy black bastard." But if you're Irish he shouts "Come on you lazy Irish bastard," or if you've got red hair "You lazy red-haired bastard." It's all the same you see, it doesn't make any difference because it's only his way of identifying you.

I've been in four years, I'm twenty, and I joined from school at sixteen with five 'O' levels. I don't know that I had any other ideas about doing anything at all. I come from St Kitts in the West Indies, I come over here with my mother when she was training to be a nurse. I don't know what it was, she kept moving around and before long I ended up in a children's home in Hertfordshire. I think I must have been a problem to her with her training, because that's where I stayed all the time. I did see her a bit, but not very often: she seemed to have a lot of different you know what I mean, men friends. And then after she got her qualification finished she met another gentleman, a white gentleman, and she went back to St Kitts with him. I haven't heard of them for quite a bit now, but I should imagine they're OK.

The Army's my family, and I think I'm going to stay in it for quite a few years yet. It's a very good life, and I enjoy it: I've lots of good mates and we have a good time together, a lot of laughs. I've got a girlfriend, but we've no ideas of getting married. I don't think it's a very good life for a young woman to be married to a private soldier, and anyway we're going to Germany at the beginning of next year. So it would be a big responsibility to take her away from her home and family here and ask her to come and live with me over there. I think I'm best where I am at the moment, which is living in barracks. I've got a nice car, the money's not too bad for a single man, and everything you want is found for you. They give you the feeling they're pleased to have you with them, your mates I mean, and I like that. I was a bit of a weedy lad when I was in the children's home, you wouldn't have recognized me compared with what I am now. I've shot up in height and I've put on a lot of weight. I do weight training and running and I play football and I go swimming, and all these things have built me up. Last time I went to see them at the children's home and at first they didn't recognize me. Then my auntie, well I call her my auntie but we all do that, she's the you know House Mother, she said to me "My word Geoff, you're the tallest man in town!" I was pleased about that, I could see she was very proud of me. They gave me a terrific time at the children's home when I went back, a big tea with all the kids sitting round and me at the top of the table, I'd put my uniform on for them and it made me feel terrific.

If you're a soldier, it makes you hardened, but in a good way, do you know what I mean? It teaches you how to remain calm if you have say an accident in your car, or if you miss a train and have to spend a night in a strange place when you're on leave. It's not just physical toughness, it's more like giving you confidence and the feeling you can get by on your own without needing anyone else to help you. When I was a small boy I was very shy and nervous, and I didn't like school because they were always picking on me, especially because of my colour. They used to think that I was some kind of inferior person because I was black, but you don't get that from your mates in your platoon. It doesn't matter what colour you are, if you're a good soldier and can do the job, that's all that matters. I really think it's very very good, the Army. People think it's still like that programme they see on the television, with screaming sergeant majors and all the rest of it: but it isn't like that at all. Most of the lads are quiet, and if you do your best you'll be OK. I suppose my greatest ambition would be the big one: to be a sergeant major and have a crown on my sleeve, to be what you might call the law enforcer of a company. It's only a dream though, there are too many courses – and anyway it's all too far away to think of at my age. I'd be delighted just to make sergeant, that'd be quite enough for me. Even if I don't get that far, I've still gone a long way: I've got the respect of people, and I feel I belong.

ii. Going out of my way:
Joseph Smith, corporal

— Me and the wife got married last year, and so now we've got this nice quarter here on the barracks estate. I work in the office there: it's hard work, there's always a lot to do, but that's what makes it interesting because we're dealing with so many different things. At present it's really just like any other ordinary nine to five job, with most weekends off except the odd one now and again. So I'd say the wife and I are both very happy.

There was a time about a year ago when I had to make the choice of whether to leave, or sign on for another six. I asked Elsie what she thought and she said "Stay in and we'll get married," so that's what I did. I'm twenty-seven and I've been eight years in the Army: before that I had a lot of dead-end jobs, waitering for a time, working in a hotel kitchen, with a firm of shop fitters doing a menial labouring job, that sort of thing. I felt I'd got no purpose, I was going out of my way if I can put it like that. I didn't know what way to go, all I knew was I wasn't going anywhere. I suppose there's a lot of black lads like me, and I'm not saying the Army would be right for them all: but it's a good life and a decent life, and it gives you the chance to make something of yourself.

There's a bit of colour prejudice, but I shouldn't think it's any more than you'd get in any other walk of life. I don't let it bother me. I was brought up by my mother and father to not react to remarks when I heard them as a child round where we lived in south London. Then when we came up to Bedfordshire for my father's job, it wasn't too bad, not as bad as it is in London anyway. Officially it doesn't exist in the Army, and the officers don't show any signs of it towards you. Or perhaps they cover it up better, I don't know. But you will occasionally get something that's a bit nasty.

The sort of thing I mean is like the other day in the next office to the one I work in, and the door was open in between. There were two sergeants in there and they were carrying on a conversation in a loud voice. They knew I was in the next room, and they were talking like they were just to make sure I heard it. What they were talking about was a new person who was coming to work in the office next week, and one of them said to the other 'I hear he's a coloured gentleman." The other one said "Black, do you mean?" And the first one said "I mean he's a fucking nigger." Stupid men, but you could come across people like that anywhere. I'm quite sure that sort of thing would get somebody reprimanded if one of his superiors heard it, but as far as I'm concerned the best thing is to ignore it. I'm just as good as they are: if they think they can get me down with language of that sort they're mistaken.

Everyone I've talked to says that corporal is the best rank you can have, and I'm very happy with it. A lot of my work is driving – I do it for the commanding officer, and I'm also a driving instructor as well as doing clerical work. So they're making full use of my talents, I don't think anyone could say they weren't getting their money's worth out of me. This is the best thing I like about the Army, and because it's all people who've volunteered it's not over-manned. They find out everything that everybody can do, and get as much as they can out of him. This means you don't have a lot of hanging about and passing time, and it makes you feel whatever you're doing is something useful. I play a lot of sport, I'm into squash and badminton, and swimming too. I've travelled a fair bit already – Germany, Ireland, Cyprus and Belize – and I hope to do a fair bit more yet, though now I'm married perhaps it will be that much harder on the wife. Still, we talked it all through and she said she was prepared for it, and perhaps if we have one or two children and build ourselves up into a nice little family, then at least she won't be so lonely when I go away. I think it's the soldier's wife who really makes or breaks the marriage. I don't think I've got the wrong sort in Elsie, I think she's an ideal person not just for an Army wife but for me.

iii.   Wait till you see me chick:
Jack Green, sergeant

— I'm walking along this street in Leicester you see, late one afternoon and it's raining, and suddenly there's this middle-aged woman blocking my way, standing in front of me right in the middle of the pavement. And she looks at me with her eyes glaring, and she says, "Why don't all you black bastards go home? You come here and you take all the jobs and all the houses, and all you do's live on the Social, you've none of you ever done a decent day's work in your lives. So go on, clear out, go back to the jungle where you came from!"

Well me, I'd been born in Leicester and lived there all my life. My father had come to this country at the beginning of the war from Nigeria, he joined up and fought for the country in the RAF, and afterwards he settled down and had been a hard-working man all his life in the Post Office. I went to school, I never got into any trouble, and I got a job as soon as I left as a trainee metal worker in a factory. I couldn't think what to reply to the woman, I was so upset because no one had ever spoken to me like that in the whole of my life. I mean at seventeen and a half you don't have the confidence to answer back, so I just walked on feeling sort of stunned. All I could see were her eyes, and I could hear her words ringing in my ears. A bit further on, almost as though it was all like prearranged, there was the Army recruiting shop over on the other side of the street: so I went straight in and I said to the sergeant there "I want to join the Army please."

He gave me a little test they do and said I'd hear in a few days. I think it was only three days before I got a letter asking me to go to the depot for more tests. It wasn't until then that I told my parents about it, and I remember my Mum burst into tears and said "Oh no, please don't go and be a soldier." My Dad said we'd better sit down and talk it over. When I told him about the woman, he said "That's not a good enough reason for joining the Army. You should only become a soldier if you want to make a career of it, not just because some stupid bloody person shouts at you in the street." That night I talked it over with my girlfriend and she said the same as my Dad. She was white, by the way.

But I wouldn't let any of them put me off, and I went to the depot and took my tests and passed them, and it was only a few weeks after that that I went off for my basic training. What they do there is what they call "beasting" – they bawl and yell at you from morning to night and give you one hell of a time. If you ever had any sensitive feelings about being black, that's the place where you either get rid of them or you give up and emigrate. It's "Nigger", "Coon", "Wog" and everything else you can think of. You get as thick-skinned as a rhinoceros, and from then onwards nobody can ever make any impression on you again by calling you that sort of thing. I liked the whole thing at the depot, they want to see how physically and mentally tough you are. I've always been a big lad and I knew they weren't going to make me crack, and they didn't.

My first posting was straight to Cyprus, lots of lovely sunshine: then I went to Kenya on exercise, and that suited me as well. Then Germany and Northern Ireland. Finally I ended up back in Germany again, and that was when I asked my wife to marry me and come with me, which we did. We've both taken the attitude all along that we ignore remarks. She gets more than I do, I think, but we feel that to pay any attention to the problem of mixed marriages would be to acknowledge that it was a problem, which we don't. The Army doesn't recognize that it is, no one's ever made any remarks of that kind to me when I've taken my wife to mess functions, but naturally on the whole you get a better type of man as a sergeant and I don't think it could happen.

The biggest thing and the most important thing is that you don't get on in promotion in the Army as a favour. There's only one way you get up from one rank to the next, and that's by doing the necessary cadres and passing the necessary exams. It's the same for you as it is for the next man: and he knows if you've got three stripes on your arm, you've earned them. You didn't get them for creeping to someone in authority, you didn't get them as a favour, you got them the same way as everybody else did. So I'm acknowledged for what I am, a man, a professional soldier of my rank. My colour doesn't come into it and is absolutely unimportant.

I've often wished I could go back and see that woman and listen to what she said again if she saw me in civvies. And you know what I'd do? I wouldn't be angry and I wouldn't be nasty, I'd just give her a friendly smile and say "Wait till you see me chick." It would be lovely if life was like that, wouldn't it?

iv.   Having a quiet laugh: Roger Dawson, staff sergeant

– I sit at my desk here, and when someone comes in through that door he sees not a black man but a very senior rank NCO. And I know that unless he's an officer, he envies me my position: but I'm an example to him of what can be achieved, and especially if he's another black man. You won't find many people in positions of authority as high as mine in any other walk of life in the country. It's certainly the top of the middle management level, and I bet there aren't that many in industry or anywhere else.

I'm thirty-eight years of age, and I shall do another five at least and then perhaps apply to go on the long service list which would see me on until I was fifty-five. I'm looking forward to a house and a pension, which I shall get so long as I don't commit any serious misdemeanours or do anything stupid, and I hope I'm not being too much of a bighead when I say it makes me proud.

I was born in British Guyana, and when I think of my time there I can't help it. Thinking about what my father said to me and my brother, I can't help having a quiet laugh. "You two," he said, "you'll never do any good either of you, because you won't work." When we got here we went to stay with one of his sisters, and neither of us has ever been back home since. My brother has done very well for himself too: he's a more studious type and now he's a teacher, he's not a rough toughie like me.

I might be sitting here nice and quiet now, but you ask some of the lads who went through the depot when I was there training them, and they'd tell you I was the biggest bastard they'd ever come across in their lives. That was one part of my Army career I enjoyed, well not more, but at least as much as any other. I've got a really mean sadistic streak in me, and I could beast as much as I liked to my heart's content. I mean imagine it: I'd had it in my time, and then I had the opportunity of going back doing it to others. And they all had to take it from me, a black man, and they couldn't say one single word in protest about it. A real horrible character I was. Mind you, some of the lads we used to get through there, they'd make your hair stand on end. They'd come in the Army because they thought they were hard men, and they thought that was what the Army was all about. So the first thing you had to do was break that down, and replace their stupid mindless thuggery with proper values and virtues like neatness and tidiness and decency. It was very satisfying, not in a nasty way at all: to turn a young hooligan into a self-respecting soldier, to keep the toughness in him but to train and direct it properly, it was really challenging.

No, I don't think I've any chance of a commission at all. Obviously my ambition is to go on and be RSM, and I think one day I might achieve that, but no more. Because though I'd argue there's no colour prejudice as such, I've still yet to come across a black officer anywhere in the British Army. I personally don't believe it could happen. I think I might perhaps eventually try for a commission, but they have ways of diverting you or keeping you waiting if they don't want to do something, and they're very skilled at it. Another generation might see things differently, but there's still so much old-fashioned baloney at officer level that I can't see a black man being admitted to what they regard as a very exclusive club. Mind you, if it's going to happen, it'll be in the Infantry. But if it's going to happen . . . that's the thing, isn't it?

8 Up through the Ranks

i. *Never in my wildest:*
   Tom Edwards, captain

ii. *Conservative Conservative:*
   Walter Davies, lieutenant

iii. *Taking the Queen's shilling:*
   Bert Price, major

i. Never in my wildest:
Tom Edwards, captain

– Oh never in my wildest, no, I could never have dreamed of
anything like it. That I'd be sitting here in the officers' mess, having
tea brought to us on a silver tray by one of the waiters, how could I
ever possibly have imagined it? Leaving school at fifteen without so
much as a single "O" level or CSE to my name – and to have come
all this way, well if anyone had suggested it that this is where I'd be
when I was forty, obviously I'd have thought they were stark staring
mad. And quite apart from that, the places I've been to and the
things I've seen: all that side of it as well, that has to be mentioned.
An absolutely wonderful career, an absolutely wonderful life,
and if it finished tomorrow I'd say every moment of it had been
sheer happiness. Mind you, I've no intention of finishing it tomorrow – I want to go on for the full term, another fifteen years if I
possibly can, which should see me safely up to major I should
think.

I was working when I left school for a wholesale fishmonger on the
docks at Yarmouth. I was the eldest boy of a family of six children,
and my father worked for the railways, so there wasn't much money
about I can tell you. One afternoon on my way home I passed a
park, there was an Army recruiting tent in it: so I thought I'd stick
my head round the flap and have a look inside. I did – and that was
the end of me. Or I ought to say, shouldn't I, that to be more truthful
it was the beginning of me. There was a big sergeant there but
nobody else, and he'd obviously got plenty of time on his hands. He
asked me what branch of the Army I was interested in and when I
said I didn't know – which I didn't, because I'd no idea what
branches there were – he said, "There's only one proper part of the

Army my lad – and that's the Infantry, if you want to be a proper soldier."

They gave me a little test which I don't think I did very well at, because I certainly wasn't very bright or clever. But it was good enough for them, and after only a week or two I got a letter to say report at the depot for training. They put you through it a bit there to see if you're going to be put off, but I wasn't. I palled up with some other lads and we all made a joke of it together, and then in due course I was sent to join the battalion which at that time was at Felixstowe. My very first posting, I'd only passed out of the depot a few days, was when we were rushed off to Stansted Airport where we had to pile on to planes. It was only after we'd taken off that I found out where we were going – to British Honduras which is now Belize of course. I'd never even heard of it, I thought it was in Africa. When I got there I was sure it was in Africa, it was several weeks before somebody showed me a world atlas: the sergeant major had one in his office, and he pointed out to me where I was. In due course, after about nine months I think, I came back here: then did two years in Aden, then to Celle in Germany. When I got there I wrote to a girl I'd met in Lowestoft one day at one of my cousins' houses, and I found out her father was already in Germany because he was in the Army as well though not the same battalion. I wrote and said why didn't she come over to see him, and perhaps she and I could see each other at the same time. The long and short of it was that she did, and after a few months when I'd had a bit of leave and met her family back in England, we got married. By then I was a corporal. And then we went to Northern Ireland for a while, then Cyprus for a year, back to Northern Ireland again, back to Germany, England then for about another year, no I beg your pardon, that must have been about eighteen months, a spell as an RSM in Germany, and finally I was commissioned after eighteen years' service.

I've never had the faintest inkling after any other girl but my wife, and that's the truth, never in my life. We have two lovely grown-up daughters, and to me life is absolutely perfect. Without a question of a doubt I married exactly the right person: it was a help that she knew something of the life, coming as she did from an Army family. We've had our separations and we've had our times together, and I would say that probably it's worked out at about half and half. But we've always said that our marriage has been like a series of honeymoons, and it has been very very nice.

My wife is a wonderful person she is, when it comes to looking after the family, the house, budgeting the money and that sort of thing, and we've never had any kind of financial worry ever in our lives. One of the principal reasons for it is that my good lady has never agreed with buying anything we couldn't afford. It's never been the case that we've got something and thought we'd pay for it later: the money has had to be there, and all through our marriage I don't think we've ever had more than about three things on the hire purchase – a car at one time, before that a washing machine, and I think once some years before that a three-piece suite.

It was one of the lads who'd joined up with me and was in that first group in the depot I was telling you about, it was him being promoted lance corporal that set me thinking. He was no brighter than I was, and as I've told you I wasn't very bright educationally either. But I thought if he could get a little bit of authority given to him and get his foot on the ladder as it were, then there was no reason that I shouldn't. The main thing to me has always been that I wanted to get on: one step at a time, I've taken it like that, like the football managers say "We take each match as it comes." That's how I've taken promotion. But I've had to work very hard to get through all the exams. For example to get up to full corporal I had to have at least a third class certificate of education, and I can tell you it was a hellish hard thing for me to do because learning is not something which comes easily to me. As time's gone on, exams have got a little bit less difficult, but my writing is still not very neat and my arithmetic is terrible. The man who invented the calculator did me a very good turn, I can tell you. But I think I'd say it's mostly a matter of enthusiasm. After a bit you start to feel to yourself "I'd like to take this course or that course just to see if I can do it," and the older you get the less self-conscious you are about failing. If you do fail, you just put it behind you and then try again the next time round.

Some people think Army officers are a special class of people, or rather that Army officers think they are. They're very blessed and lead idle existences because they're not fitted to do anything better, and that sort of thing. Well, I'm an officer and I think I've been amongst one of the fortunate people in this world, that's true: but I've worked bloody hard to get where I am. Nobody gave it to me, and I don't owe it to my Daddy or anything of that sort. I haven't found the other officers to be at all snobbish towards someone like me who's come all the way to here up through the ranks. I was a bit

apprehensive beforehand that they might be, but I told myself I'd
got where I was because of what I was, I was too old to change and
people must take me as I am. There are still a few silly young officers
who talk as though they've got a bag full of plums in their mouth.
Well, I don't have disrespect for them, a lot of them can't help the
way they speak: as far as I'm concerned if they're good hard-
working officers I respect them for that, and if they're only there
because their father's a brigadier, I tend to look on them as people
who've missed out. They come from backgrounds where they sat
down at long tables for dinner when they were children: in my
family we more often than not had fish and chips off a newspaper. I
don't see that that gives them any kind of superiority, but sometimes
some of them think it does. This is not the sort of thing you need
waste any time worrying about if you're an officer. I'm glad to say
you're judged only on your work, on whether you have leadership
qualities, and whether you're polite and well behaved. That's
something, how to behave in public, that I've learned entirely in the
Army: confidence and that sort of thing. I know I could go anywhere into any situation, military or social, and never be out of my
depth. I never went to Sandhurst, and I've never felt that put me at a
disadvantage in regard to others. I've been a captain for four years
and I have another four to do to my majority. One step at a time: I
know I shall be a major in due course, and then we'll see how far I
can get after that.

What I've achieved is something I feel I've the right to be quietly
proud about. I sometimes look back and think if I hadn't gone into
that tent in the park on my way home that day, about as far as I
could have hoped to have got at this stage would perhaps be a
foreman in a factory. But even more likely I think I'd be facing
redundancy: perhaps even already out of work. I've no criticisms to
make of the Army life. I'd say it wouldn't suit everybody, but in my
case I happened to take to it.

ii. Conservative Conservative: Walter Davies, lieutenant

– I've been in the Army now for twenty-one years: I joined when I was nineteen, and my last job before was a milkman. Well that's giving it rather too grand a description: I was a milk roundsman's assistant in the small village in Essex where I was born and had grown up. I was living at that time with one of my aunties, my Mum and Dad had split up, and they had three children, two girls and myself, and we were all farmed out to different relatives, in my case from about the age of nine or ten. I wasn't specially good at anything at school, I seem to remember the only thing I was good at was arithmetic: so when I left I didn't have educational qualifications or much in the way of job prospects. My uncle and aunt were keen for me to go on and get some kind of a training at a technical college, but I wasn't: I wanted to get a bit of money in my pocket like all the other young lads I knew. I worked at a garage for a while as a mechanic, I think at one stage I even inquired about joining the fire service. Altogether I had about six or seven different jobs, none of them with any great prospects of advancement to them.

One day I saw an advert in the paper about a career in the Army: the usual thing, not much different from those that still appear. I cut out the coupon and sent it in, and to my great surprise about a week or so later a corporal in uniform came round to the house with all sorts of pamphlets and information. He gave me a railway warrant to go to the recruiting office which was I think in Colchester at that time, where I took what used to be called a tick test, that's where they give you a list of possible answers and you tick the one that's right. Then I went to another centre for a couple of days, and ended up like everybody else does at the depot.

I was there for a few months, hoping to go abroad and see all the exotic foreign places they tell you about in the advertisements, but my first posting when I joined the battalion was to Northern Ireland. This was long before the troubles started and it was pretty uneventful, except I was away from home: and I used to write exaggerated letters back to my uncle and aunt telling them about all the adventures I'd been involved in. None of them were true, so maybe I could have made a career for myself as a writer of fiction.

Then we went to Berlin for a couple of years. I came home once or twice on leave, but I found when I came back to the village where I'd been living before I'd joined up I'd got no friends any longer. All the chaps who'd been the same age as me had gone off to do different things, just as I'd done. In due course I became a corporal, and then I came back to this country. I'd had a steady girlfriend ever since I'd gone away, and we got married then. Not long after that I had to do six months in Cyprus: this again was before the big troubles, and then only a short time after I got back my wife had the first of our two children, our daughter. Then it was back to Germany again, to Paderborn: only that time we had a quarter, a house, and we enjoyed that very much. After about seven years I was made a sergeant, which I would say is about the average length of time, then I came back to England and worked for a spell of about two years myself as a recruiting officer.

Let's see, I have all this written down to the exact day and date in my diaries, but I don't have them with me here so I'm having to remember them as best I can in order. Catterick, Cyprus, a Northern Ireland tour again, then I believe to Kenya for a couple of months of training, then on an accompanied tour to Belfast, and finally back in England with the battalion training junior soldiers down in the south. Eventually RSM, and then off to Belize and Cyprus.

I'm in till I'm fifty-five, and hopefully I'll get to major. A very few make it as high as lieutenant colonel, but although obviously I'd hope to get up to that rank, I'm not relying on it. I didn't find the change from RSM to officer to be at all difficult, because being the RSM you're quite lonely in the mess. There's only one RSM and that's you, and people are a little bit – well I won't say frightened because that wouldn't be the right word, but a little bit chary of socializing with you. It's very difficult if you've just given one of the sergeants a bollocking for something, he's not all that keen on coming and having a drink with you when he sees you sitting up at the bar. My view is that you can't give orders and shout at people unless you know exactly what it's like to take orders and be shouted at yourself. I suppose if I come to think about it, you know, I'd say I had more friends when I became an officer, joining in the mess life there with officers of all other ranks, than I had when I was one of the other ranks, and particularly when I was RSM.

As early as lance corporal I knew I wanted the Army to be my career. It was the first thing that gave me any point and purpose in life, and it's stayed that way ever since. Sometimes when I go home now to see my aunt and uncle, when I go with my wife in our smart car and we take our two well-educated, grown-up children . . . well, I wonder what'd have become of me if I'd gone on as I was doing. I've had a much more interesting life, I know that. I still see people where I lived and they never change from one time to the next, nor have they changed very much at all really since I knew them long ago. Every day in their lives is the same, they eat the same food all the time, have their same holiday in the same place, watch the same TV programmes. In the meantime I've been all over the world and have become somebody and have made something out of my life. Me and my family have a good social standing, good money and security. Particularly since being commissioned: it's become a completely different life style. You mix with a different type of person: and it has to be said a better type of person than you've been used to. Most of the men I mix and work with are from public schools or universities, and at first I felt a bit awkward about this. You get the odd bit of snobbery but it's much less than it used to be, because a lot of the officers themselves are not from a snob social background. In the Infantry in particular this is true.

I like my work, I like my responsibilities. I'm what is called the Families Officer, which means I've got something like three hundred wives I'm responsible for. It cuts down on my travelling a bit, it means that when the battalion goes away I stay here in England to look after the families. It's not something you can have any training for because no one else except an experienced soldier understands the problems of soldiers' wives. There are certain rules and regulations and standards that are expected, but so long as they come up to those they can rest assured the Army will always look after them. A lot get married too young in order to get themselves a quarter, and the reality of babies and moving, or of husbands going away, soon sorts them out. You soon get to know those who've got what it takes, and who are the weepers and complainers. But here I've got the advantage of having experienced upsets and what we call "turbulence" myself, as has my wife. We know, and I try to pass this on to the others, that if your husband's in the Army if the Army says you've got to go, then you've got to go: there's no arguing about it, you have to put up with it as best you can. Self-discipline is the thing, not only for soldiers but for their wives. You've also got to be, what shall I say, a bit conservative in your attitudes. By that I mean abide by the rules and do as you're told, keep a good family and good standards, and maintain law and order. After all, when you get on in the Army you swing away from the mob in every sense. You become part of the Establishment, and for someone like me well naturally you're proud of it. I'm not only a law and order man: but I'd say I was someone who liked things to be just so, and to go on in the same way as they've always done – as part of a tradition, part of a heritage if you like. Therefore I would say in addition to what I said a little while ago that I find myself to be quite naturally and without effort a conservative Conservative.

iii.   Taking the Queen's shilling: Bert Price, major

– I would say it was the Coronation that did it. I'd gone into the Army the year before to do my National Service, and I didn't like it one bit. But something happened to me as I think it did to a lot of other people at that time. There was this very pretty young woman who was our new Queen, and it stirred up all sorts of feelings inside people. Later on they started to call it "the new Elizabethan age" didn't they, in the newspapers? I don't know that it ever turned out to be exactly anything of that sort: but I don't know if you remember, there was definitely this feeling of excitement and national pride about. Well I was a young man and impressionable, and I think it was the way that people looked at you when you were in uniform, though God knows it wasn't a very smart uniform in those days was it? However, that was it. I was in the middle of my national service, and I inquired about being a regular soldier. I'd hardly finished my basic training I think, but that was how it came about that I found myself taking the Queen's shilling.

I'd been left school for four years and I was then nineteen, coming up to twenty. I'd no "O"s or "A"s or anything of that nature: all I'd done was labouring jobs around Leicester where I was born. If you work it out, good grief I've been in haven't I for more than thirty years? Well then there can't be any argument about it, that definitely makes me one of what they call "the old and bold", eh?

Being a soldier, there's nothing like it you know, not in any other walk of life. You can be a policeman, a miner, a nurse, and in all those you give service to the public but basically you're free. Whereas in this life you are and you've got to be entirely dedicated. You'll have situations say in a street or on a mountainside, and suddenly crack crack crack go the guns and they're aiming at you. That body of men, their lives are entirely in your hands and you're as reliant on them as they are on you. You tell them what to do, that's what they're looking to you for, and when you tell them where to go and how to deploy and how to respond to the situation, if you make the wrong decision a lot of those men could get killed. I suppose in all my career I've only been in that kind of situation where someone's been shooting at me, a total of about twelve times altogether – in Ireland, in Aden, and we had a couple of dust-ups with the Eoka lot in Cyprus. You get a little bit of headiness out of the situation, you do, because that's what you've been trained for. You don't feel frightened, you feel excited. This is the test: are you going to come through, are you going to get them or are you going to do something damn stupid and let them get you? You go cool and thoughtful, like you're trained to. But you're disciplined and your men are disciplined: it's no good you all rushing round like a bunch of trigger-happy hooligans. You know you're in danger and that you're going to have to fight your way out of it. In a sense it's like thoroughbred racehorses in the Grand National: they go round the course and they jump every obstacle, some fall and don't get up again, and others carry on right through to the end. It's a strange feeling of excitement that you can't describe to someone who's never been involved in it.

That's what it's all about really, and the difficult part is keeping yourself and your men mentally alert and up to scratch every moment year after year after year, so that you're all in peak condition the moment you're called on to fight. You hope it's never going to happen, but you know that if it does you're going to

respond in a way that a soldier should. We saw that clear enough in
the Falklands, didn't we? Their soldiers, poor sods, were a lot of
untrained unhappy lads who didn't want to be there, and didn't
know why they were. By comparison ours were highly trained
professional men, they weren't looking for a scrap so much as there
to do their job, which was to turf the other buggers out because
they'd no right to be there. And that's what they did, and they'd
every right to be proud of themselves: and the only unlucky ones
were those of us who weren't fortunate enough to be asked to
go.

A multitude of happy memories is what I've got. Being presented to
the lovely Queen Mother, being presented to Princess Margaret,
Princess Alice, and lots of other important people. Having them
here in the mess and entertaining them. That's really something for
a man to be able to say, particularly a man coming from a
completely working-class background like I do, and a father who
knew nothing but poverty all his life. He'd have been very proud of
me, my old man would, if he'd lived to see me get my commission.
My children have grown up and married, and they've been proud to
see it too, or I hope they have. Two sons but neither of them has
chosen to follow in my footsteps. That's their right and their
privilege and I've never tried to bring any influence to bear. After all,
they've both got very good educations, they've both got degrees,
one's an engineer and the other one's in town planning and that sort
of thing. Two fine boys, and without being in any way critical about
it I think it could be said that they wouldn't have the opportunities
in the Army that they have with the qualifications they've got in
civilian life. I'm a great believer in tradition and in some respects I'm
sad that nobody's in the Army carrying on the family name, but
there you are. I've never for a moment regretted being a soldier:
situations, but never being a soldier. Except perhaps just once in the
cold on a mountainside in Cyprus, where one of my mates had been
killed the day before. I began to think – just briefly mind you, it
didn't last long – that being a soldier wasn't all that wonderful a
job.

The part of my career I liked the least was immediately after I was
commissioned, when I was made the Families Officer. It seemed to
me to have nothing to do with the things I'd been trained for. I had
to sit in an office all day long, and when the men came in one after
the other saying they couldn't pay this bill or that bill and they'd got
themselves into a mess, I had to get them to sit down and we'd try

and work out how they could get themselves out of the mess. Most of them were stupid idiots who'd entered into arrangements to buy motor cars and all sorts of things like tape recorders and hi-fis and televisions and God knows what, none of which they could afford. You felt like putting a rocket up their backsides and saying "For God's sake, man, how on earth did you get yourself into such a stupid bloody mess?" Or even worse was when the men were away, and you got the women coming in with all their complaints and expecting you to do every little thing for them. You'd be amazed, you really would, at the number of trivial complaints you got from wives. Things like saying they couldn't go shopping because the bus went into town at the wrong time, and could we lay on a special bus three times a week to take them there. Or there was a woman once, you'd scarcely credit it, she came in and said she wanted to ring her mother in Scotland and she'd got no change for the telephone and could she have a pound's worth of silver: and then when I gave it to her, she just said "Thanks very much" and walked out with it. When I remonstrated with her and said if she didn't give me the money I'd see it was docked from her husband's pay, she just looked at me and said "You do that then." The paperwork there was as the result of that, I can't tell you. It was a job I didn't want and I wasn't cut out for, and I was very glad when somebody else took over from me and I went on to become Quartermaster instead.

There's no trouble about snobbery nor any of that kind of nonsense. We just don't have it in our mess at all. You'll get the young whippersnapper comes in sometimes fresh from Sandhurst or wherever, and he'll start showing off and trying to be clever and saying things he hopes will make him shine in front of the others. You say something, give your considered opinion about something, and they'll say to you after they've only been in the mess a fortnight "I don't quite agree with that." I look at them, I say "What makes you think you're entitled to disagree? Go on, you just tell us what makes you think you've a right to come here when you've only just arrived, and disagree?" That usually shuts them up. I'm afraid myself I've not much time for what I call these chocolate soldiers, they're chocolate soldiers with cream centres too. When they've got in as many days as I've got hours, then they might have a right to their own opinions.

Mind you all this is symptomatic of the modern Army isn't it? I went in the lads' canteen the other day at lunchtime, I had to go to see someone, I think it was the sergeant in charge. Do you know those boys had a choice of seven different meats for their dinner?

Five hot and two cold. Good God, you know, in my day the only choice you had with your meat was to eat it or leave it.

So summing it up for you I'd say I like to think I've been good for the Army because I owe it a lot, and I know the Army's been very very good for me.

9 People like Us

i.   *Honoured by service:*
     Harold Harrison, major

ii. *Young Lochinvar:*
     David Jenkins, major

iii. *I'm your man sir:*
     Douglas Gibson, lance corporal

iv. *Me and my brothers:*
     Kevin Bishop, private

i. Honoured by service:
Harold Harrison, major

– I don't think one could feel for one moment that one hadn't been
most extraordinarily privileged in two ways – in the first instance by
being who one is, born the son of one of the oldest-established
families in the land, and in the second place by being in one's
family's regiment. It gives me a quite indescribable feeling of being
honoured: I can look back through the regiment's history and find
that my forebears go back in it, in several instances in positions of
high command, for literally hundreds of years. One can't help being
very conscious of this: it is as I say one's family tradition, but of
course it carries with it a sense of being responsible for the upholding
of that tradition, of doing nothing to besmirch the family's name.
Indeed one hopes that both the regiment and oneself will have been
improved, however slightly, by one's carrying on of the standard.

To have been born to the high calling of professional militarism is
something one is proud to accept: one has been called to follow the
flag, to march to the drum, and in this sense is honoured by service. I
don't think that people like us always fully appreciate our position
in society. There are those who, if they don't exactly take it for
granted as their right, then don't always accept the duties that the
position brings. It is in a sense as though one has been designated, I
can think of no better word to describe it than that. And I would say
unhesitatingly that the designation carries duties and obligations,
and one has no other choice but to accept them and fulfil one's own
almost pre-selected, and certainly in some sense preordained,
destiny.

My father was a soldier, and his father before him. We had, indeed
we still have, a country house which I suppose one could describe as

a farm in the sense that it is the centre of a business scheme with land around it, though it's arable farming land and we have no livestock. I was my father's only son, and I know he regarded it as tremendously good news when I said to him at about the age of twelve "Father, I would like to join the Army when I am old enough." No pressure had been brought to bear on me, the decision was entirely my own, but I had the sense that he was entirely pleased with it. In due course I went to Sandhurst, as one does, and did all the things that were required of me in order to become an officer. The study and the examination were not as I recall particularly difficult: this seemed to be as I said to you the other evening, the entry to the way of life I was fitted for. I can't say I ever did give even a moment's thought to any other profession. One's family tradition is a guiding principle, and I can't imagine how strange it would have seemed not only to my father but to my mother and my two young sisters had I announced I wished to do something else. No, I've not so far married: the reason for it is that a suitable person has not yet entered my life. That there is one, one has no doubt, and I'm sure in due course we shall meet. I am only after all thirty-seven, and so there is no hurry yet: but I do certainly intend in due course to settle down. But I'm so tremendously enjoying myself in bachelordom that I am in no hurry yet to enter into the married state. When I do, there will then be the responsibility of children and so on, and I shall accept that in due course.

Ever since Sandhurst I have had the enormously enjoyable experience of living entirely in the officers' mess. It means one is carrying on the way of life one is accustomed to, and has been all the time: it is an extension of one's boarding school life, if one cares to put it that way. You live and play with the same chums you work with, and this is extremely pleasant.

The mess is really an extraordinary institution: there's a whole book to be written about it, about its customs and traditions etc., not to mention some of the characters who live in it. It has as I see it a threefold function. The first is that it is a house for single officers, and a meeting point for all officers single or not socially, and particularly when they are abroad and away from their own families. That is its first function. Its second is that it is what might be called a haven, a place of security in which are gathered the regimental chattels – the colours, the silver, the pictures, the old medals of soldiers who have passed on, and so the mess is both for their safe-keeping and for their display. Thirdly and most importantly it provides facilities for officers such as myself to live in while they are doing their duty, without having their time taken up with the domestic chores of life. They can work and do their duty, and not have to worry about who is going to clean their shoes, cook their meals, make their beds and all the rest of it. Their duty includes both sport and looking after their soldiers as well as their work, and it means they can concentrate entirely on *la vie militaire* without having to worry about what one might describe as the more distracting sides of life.

Of oneself it means that I can work in my office as late as I wish, and have no fear for instance of a nagging wife telephoning me to inquire why I've not yet come home. And it really is jolly nice, you know, to be rung up by someone in the mess who takes the trouble to say "It is a quarter to eight sir, and we shall be dining in a quarter of an hour's time." I am able to say "Thank you very much for informing me, corporal or whatever, I shall leave the office within the next five minutes. Would you please ask someone to go and run my bath." By the time I get to my quarters in the mess, the bath has been run and I can jump into it, and then change and be ready to go in at eight o'clock for dinner. But I do realize that one is spoiled in comparison with one's contemporaries in civilian life. Not everyone is in the position to have tea brought in the morning, to have one's meals provided and one's room kept spotlessly clean, a wine waiter at dinner and so on.

Having people to look after one, and who are let's face it one's servants, is not to my mind difficult to justify, because we are you see all servants. I am a servant of the Crown: I am in military service and I therefore give my liberty – and I mean this quite sincerely – so that my country can be free. Therefore in having a soldier in the mess and working in my service, one is asking him to do no more than I am doing voluntarily myself for the nation. It is one of the finest traditions of the Army, I believe, that this system should be perpetuated: because it does truly mean those fortunate enough to have the professionalism and sense of tradition which soldiering requires can devote themselves entirely to it, while those who would perhaps not make quite such good officers – through no fault of their own, I hasten to add – are in a subservient but no less an honourable position where their capabilities can be used to their very best extent. It would be unthinkable for one to feel that one had some kind of right to the privileges of Army life, or that others had no rights. But just as it is my privilege to serve the Queen and to lead my soldiers, so it is theirs to look after their leaders which in my case is me.

ii. Young Lochinvar: David Jenkins, major

– I'm quite confirmed in my mind now that although I've had a great deal of enjoyment out of this life, the time's coming near when I should seriously consider doing something else. I hope in about three years I'll be able to retire with a small pension: my wife has a job which is a good one, she's in advertising: and we've talked it over, she'd be prepared when the time comes to keep me for two or three years so I can perhaps get a degree. I do have the necessary basic qualifications, when I left school I had eight "O" levels and three "A" levels, and then I did some time at university without actually taking a degree. Most of all I think what I'd like to do is something on the technical side of engineering, and if I were lucky enough to be able to get it then some job that'd bring me into contact with people. Perhaps it might be to do with personnel management or something of that sort, so the degree I'd hope to get would be one in sociology.

I'm not in any sense disillusioned with my career, it's just that I no longer feel any particular satisfaction in doing it. It's difficult for me to say what particularly I don't enjoy without sounding as though I thought of myself as in some way rather different or superior. I suppose I'm finding more and more that the people in the Army are becoming increasingly right wing: or perhaps I'm becoming increasingly left wing, and they just seem like that to me. But there's certainly a kind of unthinking Toryism which is on the increase, and I mean by that an assumption that everything is for the best, everything in society should stay as it is, everyone gets what they deserve: and if they belong to what are sometimes called the "have-nots", then in some fundamental way it's their own fault.

When I came in the Army I was full of idealism. Perhaps to someone of your persuasion it sounds ironic that a soldier could be idealistic, but I thought of myself as some kind of heroic figure. You know, "So faithful in love, and so dauntless in war, There never was knight like the young Lochinvar." I don't know about the first part of it because at that time I was a young man who wasn't married, but let's say I'd been faithful in my fashion to three or four extremely nice young ladies, none of whom had been foolish enough to commit themselves to marrying me. I was all for the adventurous life, for mixing in with the lads, for living life to the full: I had the ability to treat exercises as though they were real, which you have to do, and if there'd been any kind of war we were involved in I don't think I'd have had any doubts about joining in with enthusiasm. I suppose the two most important experiences to me, the first of which I've actually experienced and the second I didn't, were what's been happening over the years in Northern Ireland, and the Falklands war. I've strong mental reservations about our being in Ireland any longer, and each time I've been there – I've now done a total of four tours – I'm less and less convinced that we even ought to be there. I don't feel inclined, perhaps because I'm too cowardly, to make any kind of dramatic renunciation of the Army if we had to go again: but I don't think that's going to arise anyway with this battalion. I have thought very hard though what I would have done if we'd been sent to the Falklands, because I strongly disagreed with the action that was being taken. I think most of my superiors would say, quite rightly, that feeling as I do the Army was no longer the right place for me.

In all of this the person equally important is my wife. We've now got two young children, and although she's always accepted it was part of Army life that I would have to spend a long proportion of time away from home, we neither of us really understood what that would entail in terms of the relationship with our children. We knew it wouldn't affect our own relationship but we hadn't considered any further than that. I miss the children, as I miss her: and she misses sharing the enjoyment of them growing up with me. The Army has to be everything, at least to the extent that you have to put it first, and when you don't want to any more, then this is another reason for not staying in it. We were talking the other evening and we worked out that since we married twelve years ago we've lived so far in a total of sixteen different homes or houses. I think it's beginning to unsettle the children as they grow up, and we don't want to put them in boarding school. I hope to be able to get a staff job for a short period now, and then move out.

I wouldn't want my son to follow in my footsteps and join the

Army. It'd be unfair to say he wouldn't enjoy it – that's one of what might be called the seductive things about it in this day and age, that soldiers of every rank are looked after very well. I don't just mean materially either, though that's part of it: I mean also your spiritual and mental welfare is considered. After all, a great deal of money's been spent on training you, whatever level or rank you're at. And the prospects of getting on are extremely good: they have to be, because if there's one thing the Army doesn't want it's unhappy soldiers who feel they're in a dead-end job. Considerable thought is put into what might be called the career structure, and everyone's encouraged to aim for better things. Very few men regard being in the Army as burdensome, because if they don't like it they can get out. Officers of course leave with a pension and a gratuity: other ranks have to buy themselves out, but all sorts of things are done to make that possible. The disaffected only spread their feelings among others, and the Army doesn't want this to happen, so it goes to considerable lengths to ensure it doesn't. I think you'd be hard put to find someone who was really eating his heart out to get out: he'd have been helped out before that stage was reached.

To return to myself: the chance to return to academic life and to civilian society is increasingly appealing, and I think I may very well do that. But I'd like to repeat if I may that I'm not in any way disillusioned or bitter: it's tempting to say I've "grown up", but it'd be fairer to say I've grown away from the Army.

Incidentally, because of what I've been saying, if you wouldn't mind I'd sooner not have any personal details about me included that would allow anyone to identify me with any certainty.

iii. I'm your man sir: Douglas Gibson, lance corporal

– I'm a soldier who you could say sir was very very happy to be a soldier sir. I think there's nothing better, I would recommend it to anyone. I would say to anyone sir that I'd think they was lucky if they was to get into the British Army today. You have your complete security, you have your sport and your travel, if you're a married man which in my case I am not, you have your house and all the rest of it, though my young lady and me will be getting married very shortly. Then she will have everything she wants too, and she's very ready to join the Army with me, as they say sir. Because if a man's wife is not right for the Army, then that man is not right for the Army either. I have known one or two who have got out, and in every case I would say it has been the wife that was the trouble, moaning and that sort of thing, or wanting this that or the other. The way I see it sir, if you have a wife like that you can't give your mind to your job, and you'll only end up unhappy, with perhaps your wife going back to the mother, or even something worse such as perhaps messing about while you're away.

I have now been in the British Army for seven years. I had a taste of civvy street and I didn't like that at all to be perfectly honest with you sir. I was working as a baker's roundsman, and I couldn't see I was ever going to get anywhere very far in that sort of a career, so I went to the recruiting office and they welcomed me. I'm a big lad as you see, and I'm very fit. I thought I was fit when I first started, but that's nothing to what I am now. I box for my company, and I'm being considered for the battalion rifle team. There is all this sort of sports opportunity given to you for absolutely free. We have swimming baths, gymnasium, football and cricket field, whatever you name the Army has got it and it's all there for your free use. If you are the sort who likes the outdoor life, then I would say you was

ideally suited for it. You can go on Adventurous Training – rock
climbing, canoeing, skiing – I've done everything of that sort sir,
and there is lots of opportunities all the time for you to enjoy
yourself.

I come from a very good home and a very good family sir, and they
are very proud of me being a soldier and what I've done. I've got
myself to a position where I'm beginning to get some rank and
authority, and my work which is to help run an anti-tank platoon is
very important for the safety of the country. We have a lot of
lectures and talks on the role of the British Army in the world today.
If somebody were to be asking me to write for example an essay
about it, I would say sir that the role of the British Army is to defend
my Queen and country against aggression wherever it occurs, and
that will most likely be I should imagine in Europe if the Russians
decide that they want to conquer it. It is our job to go where we are
ordered and stop them. I think that soldiers know things about these
things that the ordinary person doesn't, because it is our job to
know what we are doing and what we are fighting for. Yes sir I've
been to a number of places such as Belize in Central America where
you couldn't strictly say you were on guard against the Russians.
But all the same we went to get experience in jungle training,
because you never know where the main part of a war is going
to be if war breaks out. I have also been to Canada and learned
how to fight in mountainous country, so all in all you get a pretty
good training for anything that might crop up in my opinion
sir.
    I think the system of the British Army is the best one in the world.
You have those at the top who have been from families of soldiers
for hundreds of years: they're soldiers through and through, all
their fathers and grandfathers were generals and that sort of thing,
so it's natural they should be the same. And you also have the
well-spoken people who have got a lot of book learning and which
gives them the know-how to be officers. These are hand-picked men
and are likely to be of the very best sort. Your officers are your
people who you look to for your orders to tell you what to do, and
they are your people that you look up to as well. Whenever an
officer speaks to me I've found that he is always gentlemanly and
polite. He will ask you to do something, he'll say "Lance Corporal,
will you do so and so or such and such" and the way he puts it to
you, he makes you feel that you are doing him a favour. I always
reply "I'm your man sir": I feel I'm a position where I am an

important member of the Army if he, an officer, has picked me out to do something.

I have been very happy to talk to you sir and I am sure there is nothing secret or confidential in what I have said. Perhaps you would put it before the people concerned who will give the necessary permissions and it will be for them to decide if it is in order or not.

iv. Me and my brothers: Kevin Bishop, private

— Me and my brothers are all in the Army, there's three of us and for people like us it's a steady job but not much more. I'm in the Infantry and I have another brother in a different battalion, and then the third one of us is in the Engineers. We were all no good at school and came out with I would think not more than a handful of exam things between us, and we all tried all sorts of different jobs before we signed on. It's something that gives you security, that gives you a chance to think what you're going to do with your life, I think that's the best way of putting it. You sign on for three years, and then another period and then another and then another and so on: so if you're not sure whether you're going to like it or not then obviously you give yourself a chance to leave after a while, and stick it out until that time comes unless you want to buy yourself out. I'd say I look on it as just an ordinary job. I'm not married and neither of my brothers is. I think once you get into that you start to get problems, because there's such a lot of going away. If you're not a married man then you can enjoy it and you have no worries and nobody is worrying about you, and you can get the best out of it. Wherever you go, whatever country, you get leaves and things, what they call "R and R" – rest and recreation I think it stands for, and you get the opportunity to go and see places which you'd never have normally in your life otherwise.

The thing I go least on of all is what we call the FAF – that's the "Fuck About Factor", all the bull-shitting and the hanging around which you get, and general pissing around. There's the common saying in the Army "You there, hurry up and wait!" Well there's an awful lot of that, as well as the fact that half the time you're told to go somewhere or be somewhere or do something, but when you do nobody knows why the fuck you've been told to do it and what you're supposed to do anyway when you get there.

It can also be pretty bloody boring when you're doing guard duties and fatigues and generally running around, just because some stupid bugger has told you to do it. One example that comes to mind immediately is "Area Cleaning", which is a special favourite of one of our sergeant majors. He'll suddenly give the order that a whole area has to be cleaned – it might be all round one of the barrack blocks, it might be the parade ground, the roads inside the barracks, or it might even be the playing fields: but the whole area has to be cleaned – and by that he doesn't mean that it's got to be swept and trimmed up, he means every fucking fallen leaf has to be picked up. I don't think he does it because he's stupid, I think he does it because his idea is that an idle soldier is someone who can't be up to any good.

Me and my brothers have often talked about this sort of thing, and we've all agreed that when things get better outside we'll definitely be on our way and into decent jobs. But the way things are going at the moment it doesn't look as though that's going to happen for quite a time. Then you get the problem of people chivvying you to go for lance corporal and all that bullshit. The thing is that that means taking on responsibility and getting shouted at by those further along the line. The lance corporal is the very last man where the responsibility stops for anything: it's handed down and down, and he's the last bloke who can get the bollocking.

One of us lives in our parents' house, and two of us lives in barracks. I'd sooner I could get a house with my next brother in age, and we could perhaps have a couple of birds there to look after us, only the Army's not all that keen on that kind of arrangement. I can't say I'm all that fond of barrack life myself, the food's pretty poor. There's also that you can get jumped on for slopping around and looking untidy even when you're off duty. This doesn't seem to me to be the way to treat grown men, but you put up with it because you can't do anything about it. I knew an officer once who stopped a man outside the barracks because he didn't like the untidy way he was dressed and he screamed something at him, and this bloke came back into his dormitory and asked one of his mates if he could borrow some of the stuff off him that the officer had told him to get. When his mate said what is it, the soldier said "I don't properly know, I think it's some kind of hair spray. I think he said it was called 'S. P. Decor' or something."

You get one or two loony ones among the officers, but most of them are people who don't really know much about life at all. They're used to ordering people around and getting things done for them, and they're usually said to be those people who couldn't make a go of it outside. I don't know how far that's true, but I think it's pretty general from what I've heard from other people.

When you're a soldier, you don't really belong in the outside world. I know if I go in a pub with my brother for a drink we keep quiet about the fact we're in the Army, because if you say it to people they start giving you looks. A mate of mine was in a pub in the town here once and the landlord said to him "Fuck off, we don't like squaddies in here." He wasn't doing anything, he was only just standing there on his own. But you do get this feeling that people are a bit nervous about you, they think if you're a soldier you'll start a fight. The fact is, you've got to say it, there is more than a few soldiers who're like that, so I do suppose they've got some justification for saying it.

Me, I'd definitely sooner be an ordinary person. I don't like parading up and down, the Freedom Marches and all that bullshit. But it's true isn't it, there's just no jobs going at all outside? Last leave I had, I went to see a bloke in the building trade who I'd heard was looking for someone, and I asked him if I could have a job. He asked what I could do, and I said I was a soldier. "Well go down the boxing ring then, you'd be more use to them than you would to bloody me." I'm not going to put up with it longer than I have to though, not a minute. When I see the chance, I'm out: and my brothers.

10. Number One Top Soldier

     i.   *The Pinnacle:*
           Charles Thompson, RSM

    ii.   *Charlie Chase*

   iii. *Person to person: Mrs Thompson*

i. The Pinnacle: Charles Thompson, RSM

– I come from a farming background, most of my family have been farm workers, and none of them has any Army connection. When I left school at fifteen and a half I had no exam qualifications, and I did several odd jobs of one kind and another until I was almost nineteen, when I went to the recruiting office and enlisted. I had thoughts of joining the Transport Corps and learning to be a motor mechanic, or my second choice would have been the Catering Corps. But the man I saw was an Infantryman, and he talked me into it. I've never regretted it for a single day.

Like all of the old sweats I say that the basic training in my day was much harder than they give them now. I remember I had a lot of doubts about whether I wanted to stay in the Army. There were things like having to do a five-mile route march in full kit on a Friday before you could get a weekend off: and even that wasn't the finish of it, when you got back you then had to do a sprint across the barrack square – and if you didn't beat the sergeant major, you didn't get your weekend. The first three times I didn't make it and I thought that was no sort of life. I still do that now and again with my lads now, but it's not many can't beat me at my age.

I remember when I had my first leaves I used to show my mother how I was getting on. We rolled up the sitting room carpet, and I marched up and down to give her demonstrations of what I'd learned. My first posting was to Berlin – and it was there I came across my first RSM. He was a huge terrifying figure, a real man among men: barrel-chested and with little specs on the end of his nose, who growled at everybody. He'd achieved everything there was to achieve, he was all-powerful: and it was he who lit the spark in me and gave me the idea that one day I wanted to be the RSM too.

I was very near out of the Army almost as soon as I'd started though. After three months in Germany I was sitting in jail, doing forty-four days. I'd been in trouble with drinking and driving, and I think I was trying to prove my manhood to my mates or some such rubbish. My company commander – who's now a general by the way – he came to see me and he said "OK my boy, you've made a silly mistake. Now serve your time, work hard when you come out, and in due course I'll make you a lance corporal. But don't ever again try to prove to yourself or to anyone else that you're a hard case."

I thought about it, and I did exactly what he said. I got my head down and worked, and he was as good as his word and sent me on an NCO's cadre. After a year and a half I was a lance corporal, then a full corporal, and then after another three years a sergeant, and even then I was still only about twenty-two. I had a flair for being an instructor, so still after that I went on as many courses as I could.

Then the great stroke of luck occurred that I met and married my wife Margaret. I was an uneducated infantry sergeant, and she was educated and sensitive and delicate. She was then, and she's always been since, a tremendous influence on my life. We went out together for eighteen months, and two weeks after we got married I was sent to Northern Ireland. There was no quarter for us, and we had to wait almost another six months before we could be together. But her father had been a military man, so she knew from the start what would be involved in marrying a soldier. She doesn't like separation any more than I do, but she knows it's an inevitable part of the job.

I did a stint as an Intelligence sergeant, which mostly involved pinning maps together, and then after that I went to Cyprus. It was supposed to be an accompanied tour – that's one on which you have your wife and family, if you have one, with you – and it sounded as though it was going to be idyllic. But I was ambitious to get on, and went on course after course – and they were all back in England, so she stayed in Cyprus and didn't see a lot of me for very long at a time. However, I learned all the things which have been invaluable to me in my career: not just technical military things, but how to deal with men and how to spot the difference between one man and another and know the right way of handling him. As an illustration? Well, to one you'll say something like "You see that bucket, pick it up and take it to that tap over there, fill it up with water and bring it back here – now." Whereas with another what you say is "Just fill that bucket, son, will you?"

We have two children of our own and they're both at boarding school. This was something we talked over very carefully before we did it, because there are advantages and disadvantages. The main advantage is that they have continuity of education wherever I get sent. I think it's worked out very well. We chose the school after visiting a total of about eight and having a good look at them. Margaret being better educated than I am, she was the one who made the final judgment. I think the children are happy, at least they say they are, and they're very well behaved. We've never had the slightest problems with them, which you can sometimes get where the father is away a lot as he has to be in the Army.

Having become the RSM which was my ambition from the start, I can say with all modesty that I'm now at the pinnacle, careerwise. In each battalion there's only one RSM, he's the number one top soldier. It's something to be proud of, and I feel it especially so having started from such a long way back. But of course I'm not sitting back and leaving it there, I'd like to go on. I've applied for a commission and unless I do anything exceptionally foolish I should get that. The prospect of being an officer doesn't worry me in the slightest. I've been involved with every job there is as an infantry soldier at some stage in my career: I've already worked with all the officers in the battalion, and am on good terms with most of the company commanders.

As regards the social side of it, it's true there's still some silliness among some of the younger officers, and there are a few snobs. But I have the advantage of my wife, who gives me a great deal of social confidence. I shall only be forty-one or forty-two at that time, so there'll be quite a long way for me to go if I work hard. If I went into industry or something of that kind I couldn't get a position in any way commensurate, so I'll look upon it as a challenge and an opportunity.

If I move up out of the ranks, will I lose contact with friends I have who are ordinary soldiers? That's an interesting question to be asked and the answer to it is very simple. It's this: I have no friends anyway. My best friend is my brother-in-law, and he has nothing to do with the Army. I'm a one and only, in my position, and not on first name terms with a single person here. So that isn't going to provide me with any sort of problem at all. The rank structure is such that friends are not possible. I think at the officer level it will be easier to make friends.

ii.   Charlie Chase

— I'd say that of all the men in the battalion, soldiers and officers, the one everyone looks up to and respects is the RSM. He knows absolutely everything that's going on, he controls the whole bang shoot. If you're not an officer you feel he's watching your every move and is likely to pop up out of a hole in the ground right next to you if you do anything wrong: and if you're an officer, especially if you're a junior one, you have the feeling that he's very well aware of what you're doing and thinks you're a stupid idiot and that he could do it much better. The sickening thing is of course that it's quite right, he could.

(Philip D., second lieutenant)

— You rely on him utterly. He's the sort of man who can get you out of all sorts of trouble because of his knowledge — not only of everything to do with the Army but also everything to do with your company or whatever. The man's a walking encyclopedia, as well as a professional soldier to his fingertips. It's not his job to be liked, it's his job to be respected: but he can only get respect by earning it. And this is what he does.

(John R., company commander)

— I think he's the most horrible sadistic man I've ever met. I've seen him take it out on a bloke just for the sheer pleasure of it — have him marching round and round the square in the pouring rain with a full pack, just because he didn't like the expression on his face when he spoke to him. He does it so that everyone will be frightened of him. They're that all right: I shouldn't think he's got a friend in the world.

(Henry T., private)

— The RSM's just about the most stupid man I've ever met in my life. He's all for discipline: he shouts and screams and yells at people, he doesn't talk to them as though they were human beings at all. When he has you on parade he marches up and down trying to look at you in a way which he thinks will make you quake in your boots. He's like a character out of a pantomime, and all he succeeds in doing is making himself look fucking stupid. Everybody calls him "Charlie Chase", because he's a charlie – a right charlie – and all he does is chase people. Some people will try and tell you those days have gone for good in the Army. In that case people like our RSM ought to be got rid of, because they don't belong in any kind of modern set-up.

(*Bernard L., lance corporal*)

– I wouldn't want to be in his position, where everyone who had anything to do with me hated me. It might be all right for some, but I'd sooner have a few mates of my own than be that sort of person, that no one wants to know. OK, so I've got a bit of authority myself, but I don't use mine – least I hope I don't – in the way he uses his, which is just exercising power for the sheer pleasure of it. It's a funny system where you have an Army that prides itself on its spirit of comradeship, but that the top soldier doesn't have a single comrade.

(*Peter D., sergeant*)

– People are always going on about what a fucking monster the RSM is. I know I shouldn't say this, because it's not the thing: but I can only say he's been perfectly OK with me. He's only once ever given me a bollocking, and that was a time when I was about a minute and a half late coming in through the barracks gate on duty, and he just happened to be there coming out of the guardroom. He could actually have been a lot rougher with me than he was. But it was only words, and it had the effect of making sure as far as I was concerned I was never late again.

(*Gordon N., corporal*)

– RSMs are a funny breed. Ours is the sort – this is no exaggeration, I was there when he did it – who one day there was a fly in one of the clerical offices and he said to a man "Get that fly killed soldier." They had some fly spray, this was in the summer: so the soldier gave it a squirt on the window, and it dropped down dead. There was a second or two's silence, and then the RSM hit the bloody roof. He went absolutely raving mad at the soldier for letting the dead fly lie on the window ledge and not clearing it away, and also because there were a few drops of fly spray on the glass. Any normal person would have killed the fly himself in the first place if he thought it was all that important. But not our man, oh no.

(Les B., sergeant)

– He's got right to the top, which gives him something to be big-headed about – and by Christ is he big-headed! I think he sometimes thinks he's Lord God Almighty . . . which I suppose in some senses he is. But if he eventually gets a commission, which I presume he one day will, he's going to find he's got two problems. One is that very few of the officers will like him unless he behaves in what they consider to be a suitably humble way of someone who's come up through the ranks: and the other is that if he has command of soldiers, those who remember him as the RSM are not going to make life easy for him.

(Keith C., captain)

– He's an ignorant ill-educated boor, just about the most unpleasant person you could hope to meet. What I mean when I say that is that's the impression of himself he tries to give us soldiers. This is because he thinks this is all we deserve: or perhaps he thinks it's the only thing we'll respond to. But any man who can really think that, and come to the conclusion all his fellow human beings are a load of shit – well he must be a really stupid person. We had a lad in our platoon last year who was having trouble at home with his wife and that sort of thing, and whose mind wasn't really on his work. This was when we were in Belize, and he'd had several letters from her telling him about what a good time she was having while he was away. I think Charlie knew about this: and if he didn't he should have done. Yet he seemed to go out of his way not to help this man, but to be constantly picking on him and breathing down his neck. The net result was that the bloke had more than he could stand, and shouted when he was drunk one night as he came into the camp "Fuck the RSM!" The RSM didn't even hear it himself, but somebody told him, and so this bloke was up in front of his company commander and got a big fine. The result was when we got back to England he bought himself out straight away. So what did you have? You had the loss of a good soldier, simply because the RSM's pride was at stake, which I think is ridiculous.

(Jim L., sergeant)

iii.   *Person to person: Mrs Thompson*

– To be the wife of the most feared man in the battalion is something you've got to get used to. He doesn't really discuss it, but he'd probably say it was a necessary part of the job, he has to keep everyone on their toes and at the peak of efficiency. Naturally that's not going to make many men like him, but that's something I don't think would worry him greatly. To be frank about it he's always had that quality of making people – what's the word, wary of what he's going to say to them.

He was a sergeant then, and he was ambitious even in those days to be RSM. And he's got where he's got by being efficient, and by making sure those who worked with him or under him were efficient too. I mean there are people who've got where they've got by stabbing and kicking and trampling over others, but that's not something that anyone could accuse Charles of. He's got to his position by being good at his job, certainly not by currying favour from anyone. At times he can be frightening, and he's no great respecter of persons who are above him in rank. If he doesn't think they're good at their job he makes it clear, and he can convey his opinion just by looking at someone.

I don't think he's a bully, at least I hope not. He doesn't get personal animosities against his men. He'll sometimes come home in a bad temper, come stomping in through the front door and throw his briefcase down, and go off to have his bath without so much as a word to anyone. I just wait for him to calm down and get changed and sit down and relax, then after half an hour or so he's got it out of his system. The sort of thing which he gets into that state about is when things have gone wrong in the office and he feels it's due to inefficiency. He'll say sometimes that So-and-So will never make a soldier: this will be about some lad he had high hopes of, and who hasn't done something properly, or who say after several warnings has done something stupid and got into trouble. Charles gets angry about it, I think chiefly out of a sense of disappointment. To be a good soldier is to him the most worthwhile thing anyone can be, and he feels the man has let him down and let himself down. That's his major failing I'd say: he feels everyone should want to be a good soldier, and he can't always grasp it that they don't.

When I first met him, my father was adamant I shouldn't marry a soldier. He'd been one himself, and he told me in his opinion no soldier was or ever could be up to any good. It was a funny attitude, and when I said I'd like to bring Charles home to meet him he got quite stroppy about it. Charles was then a brand new sergeant, he'd been one for only three weeks: but when he came to my home he was very quiet and polite and respectable, and I think my parents took to him immediately. Then he went off to Germany and we wrote for a while, which I think is a good way of getting to know someone. But he didn't like it because he's always been a bit self-conscious about what he feels are his educational shortcomings. When he came back we got engaged, and he had to go to a regimental dinner on the night of our engagement party. He seemed very relieved that I didn't create about it: but with my father having already been in the Army, I knew exactly how that sort of thing could happen. There are things he has no control over that have to come first.

We got married and he went to Northern Ireland, and I joined him when there was a quarter for us. It was a nice quarter but I was bored so I got a job, I worked in an office. I can't say I was greatly worried about Northern Ireland. You were always conscious of the danger there was, and I didn't like it at times like when I was watching the television news at lunchtime and they announced as they did one day in a news flash that two soldiers had been shot very near where we lived. But it was only a few minutes later someone phoned from his office for something or other, and to give me a message that Charles would be half an hour late for his tea or something. He was letting me know in his own way that everything was all right. Strangely enough Charles was much more of a worrier than I was in Northern Ireland. One day we had a power cut at work and we all had to sit around waiting, so I didn't get home till seven o'clock instead of four o'clock as usual. Charles had worried himself sick about it, because I was late.

But I do tend to worry more I find as I get older. When he went to Belize and was away there on his own for six months, I didn't like that at all. I worried about daft things like him falling in a river and drowning, or getting bitten by a snake or something of that sort. I knew there was no danger from fighting, because the Army was just there as a deterrent.

Presumably he would kill someone in fighting, if it was necessary. I don't think he's ever done it, but I must admit I've never asked him directly. I don't think you think about that aspect at all. He has a job and you know that he could sometimes be in danger: but you think "My husband's away" or even "My husband's job involves fighting people and I pray he won't be hurt." You don't think "My husband's away shooting people," that's not how you think about it.

Because he's the number one soldier, in a way I have to be as far as I possibly can the number one wife here on the estate. I don't mean in terms of prestige and importance so much as in regards to responsibility. I feel it's my job to help the wives, well those who need it, as much as I can. But of course you don't go pushing yourself in. I've involved myself deeply in the wives' club, and I spend most of my days in work for the club. We have all sorts of social activities, arrange outings and functions and things like that, and they're particularly important when the men are away. We also have an advice centre, and we occasionally have people to come and talk to us. We're trying to get, for instance, a more modern approach to the subject of baby battering. I don't mean this is something which occurs often, but I think the more knowledge that's spread about it the more it helps people recognize situations that could lead to it, say perhaps in themselves, before they occur. It's very important not to regard it as something so dreadful that it can't be talked about, or something so wicked that the only solution is for people to be prosecuted. Soldiers' wives in many ways lead stressful lives, especially when husbands are away and the woman is left entirely on her own to try and cope with small children, and they've no one to turn to for help and advice. So it's in this sort of area we hope we can function, and it's just as important, some would say even more important, than in being just a purely social organization.

And I'd like to see the welfare side extended much further. We do operate strictly and only for soldiers' wives: if a couple break up and the husband goes back into camp, the woman's in a very difficult position. She has ninety days to leave the quarter, and it's not always possible to extend it. The local council are reluctant to rehouse her, because she and her husband may get back together or she may go back to her family, so she's in a sort of limbo. The Army tends to say "That's her problem" if she's homeless, as soon as she stops being married to a soldier. That sort of thing is particularly difficult if she's left her family and come over here to live from say Germany or Ireland.

On a person to person basis with Charles, I'd say I've had an interesting and rewarding life. We've two lovely nearly grown-up children, and we're giving them the best possible education, plus stability because they're at boarding school, that we can afford. I'd certainly like Charles to go for a commission. I think he's a bit apprehensive about what you might call the social side of things, functions in the officers' mess and that sort of thing: but it won't worry me in the slightest, and there's no reason for him to feel inferior socially to anyone else. Quite a few officers I've met, they'd never come up to my husband on any count whatsoever except that they began life with a lot more privileges, which is nothing for anyone to feel superior about is it?

11   In Several Places

     i.   *Germany*

    ii.   *Belize*

   iii.   *Cyprus*

   iv.   *England*

i. Germany

— To be here is a very worthwhile job, because we're making a positive contribution to peace. If we weren't here the Soviet Union undoubtedly might at the very least be tempted to think about coming further across into Europe and grabbing by force whatever she felt it would be to her advantage to have. My own soldiers, I know, are entirely in agreement with our being here and what we are doing, and it's not difficult to get them to see with the aid of talks and lectures and discussions the vitally important role they're playing here in Western Europe.

(Dennis T., company commander)

— Our role is to protect our part of Germany against threat from the other side. We have to be ready just in case, because we can never properly tell with the Russians. Yes I do honestly believe there is a threat. You could easily wake up one morning and find they were here, they'd just come across like that before you could do anything about it. That's why they teach us recognition of Russian arms and tanks and uniforms, so that we can spot them immediately: you need to be able to do it through binoculars, to tell whether a soldier in an unfamiliar uniform is one of our side or one of theirs. We have talks from the Intelligence people: they come and warn us to stay vigilant even if we read in the papers the tension between our countries is slackening. Well, I reckon myself a professional soldier and I go along with "Ours not to reason why": I don't spend too much time thinking about these sorts of things, that's for the higher ups and the politicians to sort out.

(Ray S., corporal)

– We're having a brilliant time here, digging trenches and roaming around over the vast tracts of empty land in the woods and forests. Exercises in Germany go at a much slower pace, you can take more care and you put a lot more effort into them. Where we are is ideal for young officers such as myself to learn their profession: we can put in attack after attack, practise withdrawal after withdrawal and all the rest of it seemingly endlessly. I'm sure I'm going to tremendously enjoy it, and I know my men are all keen and having a good time in their spare time as well.

(*Alan J., second lieutenant*)

– You can't help being conscious of the irony of the situation. Forty years ago or thereabouts we were fighting all over this land, trying to kill the Germans while they were trying to kill us. And now here we are in most pleasant surroundings, in a good deal less danger here than we're in for instance in parts of the United Kingdom like Northern Ireland. We know even though we're in some senses an occupying army, all the people here – everyone you see on the streets, the people you meet in shops, restaurants, the people whose homes you visit – they're all on our side. None of them is going to try to kill you, and you don't feel in any kind of danger if you're walking on your own or driving in the streets at night. Not at all like Northern Ireland: there you're in a totally different country.

(*Bob C., captain*)

– It's good because there's lots of nightlife, discos, beer festivals, wine festivals and that: and we get more money, what they call "Overseas Allowance" while we're here. But they work us pretty hard and put us on a lot of exercises, and hours are long: one of my mates says he's going to jack it in if it goes on much more, but I think he'd be a fool to himself to do that. We live comfortably and we save a bit, and we'll appreciate it when we go back to UK. When we go home we can drive to one of the Channel ports and get the ferry and it's quite cheap.

(*Arthur T., lance corporal*)

– The German people are a lot cleaner and tidier than what we are, they've built up all their towns again and take a pride in what they've reconstructed. They have a high living standard, higher than ours: this shows up in that all the shops shut on Saturday afternoon, so they can't be all that worried about making money. A lot of things are much cheaper here: some of the food but not all, on the other hand the clothing is very expensive. Cars are cheaper, though the insurance is very high for soldiers: that's a case of the few doing harm to the many, the stupid drunken drivers are the culprits. It's a very religious country too on Sundays, there's a hell of a lot of church bells going. I quite like it, but give me good old UK.

(*Fred K., private*)

— I'd say most of the German people was friendly on the whole, even though they're not all that keen on having us in their country. I suppose we'd feel the same if they were in England. You'll some-times get a queue at the cash desk in the supermarket where some of the older people will push in front of you: they seem to know you're English and you must be a soldier. But they might be that sort of person anyway, they might push in front of the younger ones if they didn't want to stand a long time waiting. A few of the young ones, you occasionally get remarks made at you in the streets, but this doesn't worry me: I don't understand their lingo anyway.

(*Alfred C., private*)

— Drug and drug-related offences are very few and far between but all the same it'd be foolish if we didn't take notice of them. I imagine it's probably more widespread back in the UK than among the forces here, but you do get a number of German young people who use drugs, inevitably soldiers start to mix with them and so that's how it begins. Another problem is that drugs are rather more easily available here. There are a number of cities, not necessarily in Germany itself but in countries on its borders, where people go for visits and bring drugs back in. But I wouldn't have said it was a large scale problem. If you're convicted of course you're automatically court-martialled and thrown out, and I think every soldier is well aware of what will happen to him if drugs are found in his possession. The penalties are much more severe for someone in the forces than they would be for a civilian, who'd probably only get fined for a first offence.

(*Brian D., company commander*)

— I wouldn't say it was one of our major problems, but a number of soldiers go absent without leave in Germany, who we never manage to trace. Not a large number, but more than we have in England. What probably happens is a soldier meets up with a German girl or woman, decides he's had enough of the Army and wants out, and she takes him in and looks after him, and she may well have ways and means of getting him papers. If he does that sort of thing in England we have names and addresses of relatives who we go and see as a matter of course: but if a man does that here and goes to someone we've no knowledge of, obviously we're in difficulty. Especially if for instance he's an already married man and just wants to disappear: or he might have pressing debts or something. When you think there are about 60,000 British troops in Germany it's not surprising we lose the occasional one here and there.

(Ian J., major)

— My wife didn't like it at all when we first came here, I thought we were going to have trouble. We've just had our first baby, neither of us could speak any German, and we were both scared of the language barrier. The wife thought she'd feel very isolated and out of it. But our quarter's in along with a fair number of other English wives, and there's nothing like the language problem we thought. This is a garrison town you see, so nearly all the German people here speak a fair bit of English. Up to now we've had no trouble at all trying to make ourselves understood.

(Frank T., corporal)

— I mean look at it, this quarter we're in is twice the size of the one we had in England. I came here not knowing what I was going to think, but after only a few months I like it very much. It's a much cleaner country than England, there's no litter in the streets, they keep the shops tidy and neat — somehow they seem to be much prouder of their way of life than we are. The German people are very nice: they all speak English to you, and if you ask them what the German word is they tell you and then you all have a laugh about the way you pronounce it. To my mind I'd be happy if my husband stayed here a long time.

(Sheila R., private's wife)

— I get really fed up with the Families Officer when he comes round doing his garden inspections. He says we've got to put on a good show for the Germans because they're always so neat and tidy: if you hang your washing on certain days you get into trouble for it. He says, "Look around, do you see any washing hanging on the balconies of those flats over there, just remember the Germans don't do things like that." He's a pain in the arse when he goes on like that.

(Stella C., corporal's wife)

– My parents have no resentment that I have married an English soldier. We met only three months ago, we have decided straight away we were in love and we wanted to be married. When I told my mother and father, there was great family discussion and some tears, because I think my mother thought I was going to go immediately to England and she would never see me again. When I was able to tell her we are going to live here and my husband is staying for four years, she was immediately very happy. But my father: well I think for him it is slightly different because he was in the war. He was only a young boy at the end of it, but at that time even very young boys were brought into the army. He has met my husband and my husband is not very much older than he was at that time, and he shook his hand and said to him "We are both soldiers." I am sure everything will work out, because we all want the same thing which is peace, and that is what the British Army is here for.

(Maria B., sergeant's wife)

– I've done twenty-two years and it's me and the wife's ambition when our time is up to settle here. We've had many times in Germany and we both like it. Everything's clean and spotless, and people are always friendly. There's no problem to us with the language, we struggle through because 99 per cent of the people can speak English. The wife's thinking of perhaps taking a German course: but the trouble is, what they teach you is what you might call Oxford German whereas what you really want to know is street German.

We've got at least twenty or thirty German friends among civilians who've nothing at all to do with the Army, and most of the time we've had our children here with us. Our two daughters both say they'd be very happy to settle here in Germany. My wife rather fancies a shop if we can raise the capital, and I'm the sort of person that could turn my hand to anything. Over the years we've come to feel our roots is here, more so than we've ever felt anywhere in England.

(George G., corporal)

ii. Belize

– What cheeses me off about it is we get no credit for being here, the public doesn't really know or want to know, or care. If we was to withdraw from the country next week, most people at home wouldn't be worried about it. They might wonder vaguely why we'd been here in the first place, but that would be about it. At least with the Falklands there were British people to be protected, but here there aren't, so I wonder if the British people give a fuck.

(Leslie T., private)

– To me being here is a very valuable experience, and a broadening of my thinking. We have a defined job and there's a defined enemy, even if we can't see him. Going out on patrol and operating in the jungle, practising taking up positions and the rest of it – it's all a great challenge. Even staying alive is a challenge in the jungle and not in the line of general thinking which you've had when you were at Sandhurst.

(Clive R., second lieutenant)

– They've told us there's 7,000 people just over the other side of the border ready to invade. All I can say is if they can even find the fucking border they must be brilliant, because it's somewhere out there in that jungle but it's not marked out with ribbons or anything. You can walk backwards and forwards as often as you like across it and nobody knows because you don't know yourself. They talk about the threat from Guatemala, I don't know that people here think it's any particular threat. I think they're glad to have us here because they get some of our money we have to spend, but I can't see we're otherwise any good to them, how can we be?

(Neil J., corporal)

– I enjoy being here. Parts of our job are irritating – the slowness and inefficiency of some of the local people I have to deal with – but it's a very beautiful country, with the second largest barrier reef in the world off its coast. There're marvellous opportunities for relaxation here, all kinds of water sport, fishing, swimming, snorkelling. I find the jungle very interesting and challenging too, because I've never experienced anything like it before.

(*Michael B., company commander*)

– This is my first posting. I only knew about it three days before I finished at the depot and they told me I was coming here. I asked a sergeant what it was like, and he told me everybody who came here was lucky, because it was like a tropical paradise. As soon as I stepped off the plane I went light-headed with the heat, it must have been about 115°. I've never experienced nothing like this heat.

(*Andrew A., private*)

– It's useful to my junior commanders to get away and act on their own. We have private soldiers in charge of fourteen-day patrols, and I think the officers and men will go home much fitter and more confident in themselves. There's much more fun, as well as a certain element of danger. It means one can concentrate much more on practising one's job: there's much less interference, large parts of the country being uninhabited except for the odd small tribe here and there.

(*Frank C., company commander*)

– This is a stinking dump, the most frightful place I've ever been in in my life. They have open sewers in the streets, flies everywhere all over the food and the people, and the heat is absolutely mind-blowing. I guess it's good experience for me, though Christ knows what sort of experience it is. I honestly have to say to you that I don't know what the fuck I'm doing here, I really don't. How could you explain to anyone just how dreadful this place is if they've never actually been here?

(*Arthur W., lance corporal*)

– I suppose I find the hardest thing is taking men out on patrols, because there's no actual enemy for them to look out for, and they know and I know that in all probability there isn't ever going to be any enemy here. It's very hard to motivate people: about all you can tell them is that it's great experience. One of the men in our platoon thinks he's a humorist, about twice a day he shouts out, "Russians ahead, sir!" At first everyone thought it was funny, but after he's done it twenty times our nerves wear a bit thin. I have a feeling one day I might find him lying with his mouth open and a bullet through his head.

(*Peter H., captain*)

— It's six thirty in the morning, and this is the time I said I'd talk to you because from now on it gets hotter and I get more knackered. We had a temperature of 115° yesterday, and when it gets as high as that I can feel my brain starting to bubble inside my head.

(*Len B., sergeant*)

— I can't say coming here has made me want to dash out and help the Third World. I get professional satisfaction from being here because I'm left to get on with my job in my own way. I'm seeing a new country and meeting new people: and dashing about by helicopter gives me the widest view of the whole country, and enables me to see more of it than most other people.

(*William P., major*)

— Belize, Belize, oh Belize . . . What a place, eh. This camp here, all you could say is it's a hole in the jungle can't you? Hundreds of miles of thick jungle all round you. You walk a hundred yards from here and you'd be lost from view and never be able to find us again. I think it's just loathsome,

(*Bob D., sergeant*)

— This place? Well I've been here almost six months now and the main thing I'd say is it's hot. There's no nightlife, nothing really except to watch old videos in the NAAFI and read. It's boring, and I get depressed because things get on top of me. I don't get the chance to go out, I'm just a driver. I do a bit of sport and running to pass the time, but it drags on. I don't like the heat, it makes you feel really down. One thing I do know is that I hope I never get sent here again.

(*Donald D., private*)

— That little bazaar place about the size of a telephone box you went with us, we call it "The Guat shop". It's owned by a woman who goes over to Guatemala once a week to stock up with goods and then brings them back here to sell to the soldiers for souvenirs. She's got everything from pots and pans to even dress shirts. She's one of the few people around who's got any initiative or go, and I should think she's built up her nice little business because let's face it there's fuck all else for the soldiers to spend their money on except drink and the local whores. We've all heard the Belizians are apprehensive about Guatemala coming in: but I should think there's a good number of them think that if they weren't better off, they couldn't be worse off.

(*John K., corporal*)

— Down in the town must be the grubbiest place I've ever seen. Petticoat Lane on a Sunday looks like Bond Street by comparison. There's rubbish everywhere, half-dressed kids running around waving machetes at one another, dogs, Christ it's terrible. I think most of the people are indifferent, they just look through us most times. They seem to make no attempt at all to improve themselves. I don't know what's the matter with them, they don't seem to have any self-pride.

(*Bill E., lance corporal*)

— I mean I'm a black person right? I mean the part of the West Indies that I came from as a child, we had poverty and all that, the living was a much lower standard than in England. But the poverty we had was nothing like what I've seen here. I don't know how they put up with this, I don't know why there isn't a revolution. The people must be very passive and unthinking people if they put up with this. They say we're here to stop the Guatemalans coming over the border and invading. I don't know nothing about Guatemala, but I'm sure they couldn't be any fucking worse off than they are as they are now.

(*Eric E., private*)

— Christ, the poverty wasn't half a shock when we got here, I've never seen anything like it. You might have got a bit of it on films or television, where you see these natives living somewhere in huts — but actually to come right in amongst it and realize that for the people who inhabit the country there's fuck all else, it's a big shock. The trouble is after a few weeks you stop noticing it, you don't see the ragged clothing and undernourishment and squalor, you walk through it without seeing it.

(*Norman L., lance corporal*)

— All the people you see in the jungle, living in huts on stilts, it makes you think about how lucky we are in our country. I'm never going to complain about conditions at home ever again.

(*Gary J., private*)

— The people are very poor, but I'd say that's largely their own fault because they don't make any effort over anything.

(*Cliff C., sergeant*)

— We go out to the islands off the coast now and again in a boat, they call that a keys (cayes) trip. They're like little islands in a reef. It's very pretty but so far I've only been on one because all I wanted to do when I got there was keep in the shade somewhere, I felt sick because of the heat.

(*Hugh P., second lieutenant*)

— The longest I've gone without a letter from home is three weeks, and I do miss that because time goes very slow. It's just evening after evening in the NAAFI. It's the worst place I've ever been to, it's like six months of your life cut off. I've saved some money because there's nothing to spent it on: the souvenirs in the little what they call Guat shop are absolute rubbish. I go runs either in the morning before the sun's hot or at night time. That's all there is.

(*Fred G., private*)

— This country is the most horrible country I've ever been in, and I don't even know why we're here. It's been the worstest six months I've had so far in eight years in the Army: even when I went on my leave to Mexico for two weeks it rained every day all the time I was there. This heat just gets me down and it goes on and on, I don't know how anyone does anything here at all.

(*Harold S., corporal*)

— You go on your what they call "R and R", rest and relaxation, and you can go to the Caribbean, to Mexico, or to the United States. I've been to Mexico for two weeks. I had a good time but I spent too much of my money so now I'll have to save up for having a bit in hand when I go home. I wrote to the wife telling her what a good place Mexico was and how nice it was to be there after the jungle. She wrote me a real shirty letter back, she said she was sorry I'd enjoyed any of it and how come I never took her on a decent holiday like that?

(*Jim M., private*)

— Down the road at the sea there's a bit of a place that's opened up on to cater for soldiers. The best part of it is a restaurant, well it's just a small hut really. The bloke who owns it cooks food for the soldiers and serves drinks. He's all right: if you have too much he'll give you a lift back here in his car. I wrote his menu down off the blackboard outside. It says: "Restaurant menu. Egg & Chips. Sausage & Chips. Lobster & Chips. Fish & Chips. Conch & Chips. Music. Girls, very nice."

(*Barry T., sergeant*)

— A couple of the other bars are really nothing else but pick-up places. They're not very good hygiene-wise. Some of the girls, they can't be more than eleven or twelve. It really turns me up when they come and say "Would you like to make love with me?" I don't think you could even call them prostitutes, God knows what you'd call them: they're just trying to get money from British soldiers and there's nothing they won't do for it.

(*Paul F., corporal*)

— Jesus, what a fucking country, you wouldn't wish it on anyone would you? Every living creature wants to either eat you, bite you, or give you the pox. It's fucking atrocious. And those girls down the road there at the bars: I mean I've had a few experiences in my time but them ... I never thought the day'd come when I'd pass by a chance to have a bit of hole, but I'm not kidding you, I wouldn't even look at it never mind touch it.

(*Ken P., private*)

— I drink about eight pints of water a day and I get weary very quick. I've only been to a disco once, I didn't like it. It's nothing like anything in England, all kids and little girls trying to pick you up. They most of them don't even speak English. Everyone lives in shacks with no water: if they want to pee they just do it where they are, and all along the beach there are huts on short piers out over the sea to go if they want a shit. I'd been told it was going to be a paradise, and I thought oh Christ if this is paradise what's hell like?

(*Bob D., lance corporal*)

– I don't know what a soldier says to his wife when he goes back home and he's got a dose which he picked up here. A lot of the lads, if a girl looks as though she's tempting one of them his mates'll drag him out and take him away. Specially if he's a married man, they don't want him picking up something. I've seen lads who've just arrived here and they're all excited and joking about getting down amongst the local talent as they call it. You go with them and you see the expression on their faces when they see what the local talent really is. You don't have to be much of a man to pull some skinny kid who comes up and tells you you can go round the back and screw her for the equivalent of 50p.

(*Reg H., sergeant major*)

– The laughing in the mess at tea time was when Teddy was talking about his experience last night down at one of the brothels. He said the woman he got was so horrible he didn't want her to touch him, but he couldn't think how to do it without. He was saying they were both circling round each other when she suddenly jumped up on the rickety bed stark naked and said "Give me the money or I jump on you." We were all saying whether we thought we'd be able to resist a stark naked woman, and Moley was the only one who said he wouldn't. We're all supposed to be going down there again tonight, but for Christ's sake don't tell them I told you.

(*Geoffrey R., second lieutenant*)

– It'd be unrealistic to put the brothels out of bounds. It'd only lead to trouble because you'd get men going there whatever you said. If that's what a man's got in mind that's what he's going to do. And we can't inspect them and make suggestions about improvements in their hygiene because that would be signalling our acceptance they exist. I'm afraid this is just one of the facts of life.

(*Hugh J., company commander*)

– When you go out in the jungle you stay out for a week or eight days and you have to carry all your supplies with you: in our case we took half our supplies and then a helicopter came out to us with the rest.

(*Tom N., captain*)

– This jungle here belongs to the ants and the creepy-crawlies, they don't like you coming into their territory. And those what we call "bastard" trees, the ones with big needles that stick in you if you happen to touch them, I suppose you could say it was their jungle too. It's surprising how many different kinds of nasty there are there eh? If you're on a track in the jungle and trip up and stumble, don't put your hand out to save yourself because you're almost certain to put it on one of those bastard trees. They've got two-inch-long needles all over them. I think the jungle's nasty eh — nasty nasty, know what I mean?

(Paul S., sergeant major)

— In the jungle we sleep in hammocks see, because you have to keep up off the ground away from the rats and the snakes and the scorpions and all them things. They've got some bloody great things called "possum rats", very big, big as cats: on the whole docile but they'll go for you if they're cornered.

(Ken R., corporal)

— When we were at one of the little outposts in the jungle there was an officer who found the jungle really terrifying. He'd been on the streets in Belfast, shot at, and in a hundred exercises in England. But what frightened him about here was there was no human enemy. We're trained to be on our guard against human enemies: a rifle shot, the explosion of a grenade, the appearance round the corner of a tank — we all know what to do. We deploy, take cover, put in an attack or whatever. But in this stinky sweating jungle with its snakes and animals and stinging insects, not to mention poisonous plants and trees that spit sap at you — there's nothing we've learned in training about how to deal with this sort of enemy. So this guy couldn't take it. We were both sharing the same shelter and I went back unexpectedly one day when we were about to set off on patrol. He was drinking a tumblerful of salt water: he said he'd got an upset stomach. When he was sick a few minutes later I twigged what he'd done, and I knew he'd done it to get out of the patrol because he couldn't face it.

(Steve B., lieutenant)

— They tell you officially their principal crop is sugar, but they do a much bigger trade in marijuana, they grow a lot of that. If it could be legalized it'd really set the country's economy on its feet.

(Chris G., major)

— When you look around you see they could improve their own standard of living a bit if they got some help to do something with their country. But when we go out on patrols the only thing we see people cultivating that's profitable is marijuana. It's one of their biggest exports now. We destroy their fields of it for them and it causes a lot of bad feeling.

(*Arthur L., sergeant major*)

– Drug trafficking is not a serious problem, but I wouldn't like to say how long it will be before it might become one. We include with our patrols always at least one member of the Belize Defence Force and it's his job to arrest cultivators or traffickers. It's not a very nice situation: it's nothing to do with us and that's not what we're here for.

(*John M., captain*)

– In our own way we are here to help the Third World. We're here to help the Belizian government and deter the Guatemalans. We're giving Belize a chance to build up their own country and particularly their own army, until they're more able to stand on their own feet. One can't help being aware though of the deprivation of the people. It's obvious they do need some kind of financial help: perhaps one should call it "social help". Whether that's something for the British government to do I wouldn't be competent to judge.

(*Gordon S., major*)

– Why we're here is very simple. When they got independence the Belizian government asked us to keep a military presence here to deter their next-door neighbour Guatemala from invading. But I don't know we can go on justifying it for long: independence has responsibilities and risks that people have to accept.

I believe historically what we wanted was a sort of staging-post port in Central America to give us access from the Atlantic. We took the country's mahogany which we got at very little cost to ourselves, but we didn't give the country much in return: no proper system of education, no health services, no legal system, nothing like that. There were few British settlers, which considering the heat and the lack of sanitation isn't surprising, and we invested no money in the country.

(*Derek E., lieutenant*)

– I do think we ought to be trying to do more for the people of the country and about their social conditions. Since it was once our country we have a responsibility towards them. Giving them independence and leaving it at that means nothing to them.

(*Ted T., sergeant*)

– You only need to walk around for a while before you start wondering about the millions of pounds being spent on military aid. But whose benefit's it for? How much better if a proportion of it was spent on the welfare of the people: but none of it improves their living standards, their health, their education, anything. Teach them to form a citizens' army, to defend themselves if they really do feel threatened: but it's nonsense to go on pouring money into military aid . . .

(*Ray L., lieutenant*)

– One of my soldiers has married a Belizian girl, and it's going to prove a disaster when he takes her back home. Wherever we are we always get soldiers who want to marry local girls, but I usually try and persuade them to hang on for a while: until they've known the girl six months at least, and taken her home to meet their parents at least once.

(*Leslie C., major*)

– One of my mates here, he's thinking of marrying a Belizian person. I don't reckon that's a good idea myself. Back home I know someone who lives on our estate from a different regiment, he's married a Belizian lady. You sometimes see her walking around even in quite warm weather all muffled up in a duffel coat. I suppose she thought she'd do much better for herself there than she could do anywhere here. I suppose she's right in that, but when I saw her back home as far as I could see all she'd done was jump out of the frying pan into the freezer.

(*Don J., lance corporal*)

– Where I come from, Luton, they've cleared all the jungle by now, so I wasn't expecting nothing like this place. What was it called before, British Honduras or something was it? I've heard someone describe it as one of the last outposts of the old Empire. A better name for it'd be the arsehole of the Empire.

(*Cliff G., private*)

– I shan't miss it, we've done our job here such as it is and I'm glad it's coming to its end. I was just doing my duty, going where I was sent, but I didn't agree we should have to come in the first place. But who am I to say that? That's not what my job is, my job is doing what I'm told.

(*Len H., sergeant*)

– I'm lonely and miss my family, time goes very very slow. I'm just here doing a job but it's a lousy job and I'd sooner be somewhere else. Tomorrow I'm thinking of doing something I've never done before in all my life, something right out of the ordinary: one of the blokes asked me if I would, I said "Yes all right, anything for a change." So tomorrow I'm going to play a game of ping-pong.

(*Neil J., corporal*)

iii. *Cyprus*

– Cyprus is divided between Greece and Turkey, along the line decided between them and guaranteed temporarily at least by the United Nations. So we're here for six months as part of the UN forces, helping to preserve this *status quo*. If you like, to give time for them to agree between each other how to settle their differences. We're preserving and protecting people's lives, and giving the diplomats time to sort it out. I think that's a good and worthwhile thing to be doing, and I'm sure no one could argue about the value of it.

(*H. A., commanding officer*)

– What we're doing here is trying to keep the combatants apart. The Turks and the Greeks have been fighting each other for hundreds of years, so now the UN says they've got to stop and settle their differences peacefully. We're here to keep the peace and make sure they do that, and I think this is a good job to be doing in the world.

(*Victor W., private*)

– After the Turkish invasion in which the Turks occupied 38 per cent of the island, 180,000 Greek Cypriots left the Turkish-occupied area and went to the south, and 45,000 Turkish Cypriots left the Greek area and went to the north. The Turkish armed force remaining is somewhere in the region of 30,000 men.

(Edward R., briefing officer)

– Eventually the Greeks and Turks will have to hammer out an agreement. The Turks here in the villages were having a hard time and really were being persecuted. Some of the Greek military people are former EOKA commanders: and they're a legacy of the regime in Greece of the Colonels. The Turks on the other hand are very quiet and restrained, and behave like perfect gentlemen.

(Philip B., major)

In the UN there's a British contingent, a Danish contingent, Austrians, Canadians, Australians, Swedish, and small Irish and Finnish contingents. Together they make up the UN force, and each has their individual sector. None of the other countries though has what we have, which is a Sovereign Base here. So half our force is at the Sovereign Base and the other half is with the UN: we're all here a total of six months and swap round half way through. Training-wise it's not much good, because there aren't many parts of the island we can go. But socially as far as the UN is concerned there are a lot of parties to meet the other contingents. I find the mixing with people from other countries very interesting.

(Jonathan S., second lieutenant)

– The UN in general are very pleasant people and they have a mission here. It's good for our soldiers to know they're keeping Greeks and Turks apart. Which they certainly are, they really would be at each other's throats within hours of a UN withdrawal.

(Joe R., sergeant)

– I enjoy the meetings we have, the diplomacy if you like, between one side and another. Once a fortnight we meet representatives of the Turks and representatives of the Greeks to iron out any particular problems between them in this sector. But that's only a total of something like two hours a fortnight as an arbiter.

(Graham P., captain)

– We only need, to be honest, only a very few soldiers here: I think we could manage with a much smaller force. The Turks are very strong, and I can't see the Greeks attacking them or getting back any territory if they do. I think we're not regarded as much more than

someone to complain to. We're not really needed in the military
sense: there's no adrenalin flowing, and we've got hundreds of
soldiers doing completely unnecessary things. They find it tedious,
and they don't like being separated from their families.

(*Tony D., corporal*)

– I've been a bit sickened by the UN gravy train: cars, allowances, all
the rest of it, people whizzing around trying to look important in a
pleasant climate. They're all enjoying it while they can, they know it
won't last for ever.

(*Roger S., lieutenant*)

– There's no similarity with Northern Ireland. We don't wear flak
jackets and we don't carry weapons around with us. We have to be a
lot more cerebral, a lot more thoughtful about what we do: a tough
uncompromising reaction would be inappropriate here. You
only take action of any kind after a great deal of thought and
consultation.

(*Tim M., captain*)

– What precisely we're doing here I don't know. We're supposed to
be part of the United Nations force and I did think that might mean
a few joint exercises. But so far there's been nothing like that: it's all
very boring.

(*Stanley L., lance corporal*)

– To be honest with you I see no progress towards a solution here,
absolutely none whatsoever. At the lower level, the farmers would
get on with one another, and I think the ordinary people in general
would. But the politicians: well I don't suppose I'd better say any
more about that.

(*Ralph D., sergeant*)

– I was quite excited when I came here at the prospect of peace-
keeping. But I've become a bit disillusioned in the last few months
by the political inertia on both sides.

(*Jeremy M., second lieutenant*)

– There are really no serious problems here, no one's getting killed,
no one's getting massacred. In fact work finishes at lunchtime, so
then in the afternoons we entertain ourselves as best we can with
sport and recreation. Most of the afternoons after lunch some of us

go off to practise golf or tennis, or those who're that way inclined, they can play polo. On the whole it's a rather gentlemanly sort of life that in most places has long since gone out of date.

(Mark G., lieutenant)

– We get a series of visitors out here of course, from generals down. For them it's just a holiday, combining what they call 'An inspection' which takes about an hour, then a nice little ten-day holiday on a free trip.

(Michael T., captain)

– On our sector of the UN front we have fifteen observation posts along a 35 kilometre front, and what we're doing is policing a 2–3 kilometre-wide buffer zone.

(Edward R., briefing officer)

– I'm not all that struck on being here in this observation post on the line between the Greeks and the Turks. It's only got one thing in it to me and that's boredom. Where we're billeted back in the old factory there's no telly, but just occasionally someone brings one up with a couple of videos. I don't like the island much, it seems a bit of a dump to me. This is my first time here and I hope it's the last. When I get any spare time I go for a swim or lie on the beach. We've had a few bits of training and stuff, a bit of weapons instruction, but I wouldn't say much else. We had a game of football the other day: the ball went into that field and no one would go and get it, because they're all minefields round here and you can only cross at certain places. I do three hours on duty here at this sangar, then nine hours off. I got the raw deal, I drew 3 a.m. to 6 a.m. so it mucks up the days. For recreation I go to a hotel down there along the beach: I run there, have a beer and run back. Or you can go for a meal – the people here are used to cooking for the British and you can get quite decent meals. By the side of my OP there's this hole, it's for me to jump in. If there's firing, I get in there and keep my head down. I don't expect anything like that to happen because the United Nations is keeping the peace. I don't feel that I'm doing anything very important, like I say my main feeling is boredom.

(Len W., private)

– The only ones of our soldiers who have rifles are those here in the OPs, in the sangars as we call them, which are little pill-boxes built up with rocks and sandbags. Our job here on this mountainside is to

log the activities of the Turkish forces just over there. We watch
them through binoculars and write down everything that happens.

(Terry C., lance corporal)

– The last six weeks we've been sleeping in tents on grass: the
sergeant says it's what you might call a camping holiday. I'm not
greatly struck on it. We just sit around, play cards, do our duties and
things, and then try to think of other things to do. The local girls are
very stand-offish, I think because the other UN troops who are
around here, the Canadians and Swedes, they've got a lot more
money to throw around than we have so they get first pick.

(Bert L., private)

– About the only thing different here as far as I can see is that when
we was in Belize we dug trenches, here you have to build them up
from the rocks in what're called sangars. I've been to Limassol,
Paphos, Larnaca and Troodos which is a place up in the mountains
with snow where you can ski if you want. I think it's a nice island
and I hope to come back one day and bring my wife and family. It's
all built over very much along the coast, all them big hotels, they
seem to make a special effort for holiday people. On the whole I'd
say it wasn't too bad but a bit boring in your spare time lying on the
beach or swimming: we're a long way from any town where we can
go where there's much going on.

(Harry B., lance corporal)

– I don't envy the CO his job, he's got to think up activities to stop
boredom. He wants to keep the battalion sharp but it's not easy
here. A six-month tour is more than anyone can stand without
getting utterly pissed off by it.

(Jack D., private)

– This is what, the fourth time I've been here: I've always liked being
in Cyprus even though most of the people are Greek and I don't like
Greeks. I've not learned a Greek word of any kind and the people in
restaurants, all they're interested in is our money, so they don't talk
to us very much. They've got troops from half the nations in the
world here: I know it's to stop them from being overrun by the
Turks, but I don't suppose I'd like it if it was in England and we had
foreign troops.

(Max N., sergeant)

– I'd say we have less than normal trouble with the soldiers, a few drink-related fights and bits of bother but very little. The UN line is totally dry, the CO won't allow any drink there at all. When you walk out in the towns or wherever you go you have to wear uniform: that's British uniform but with the light blue UN beret. A few places are out of bounds: usually bars where some of the young Greeks are spoiling for a fight with soldiers. Not a lot of trouble otherwise. One or two brothels but not many of our lads go into them, they haven't got the money to throw around compared to some of the other UN troops, and girls tend to favour those.

(*Don M., sergeant*)

– In a lot of places, they don't stop you going in but once they know you're a British soldier they start muttering among themselves. I haven't a clue why they should be like that. I think it's something to do with history, years back we had this island as ours and some of the older people remember it.

(*Dick R., lance corporal*)

– I like being back here. The last time was the EOKA days when old Makarios and the others were enjoying themselves. You really felt you were doing something good then: I was a sergeant, and it was one of the best postings I've ever had – lots of sunshine, lots of action. We pulled in one well-known terrorist, it really made you feel like a proper soldier. You had the occasional scrap but that was what we were there for.

(*Henry P., major*)

– I like it now but I didn't like it a few years back when we were last here, I can tell you that. You went round the streets and this was in EOKA time: and there was no way you could tell who was your enemy. You took it for granted that everyone was, just to be on the safe side. If they had a coloured skin of any sort you watched yourself. You'd be up on the rooftops in the villages or towns and you were very vulnerable: and the trouble was you had to wait for somebody to shoot at you before you could return fire. Grenades were coming over high walls as you were walking along the street, your checkpoints were mortared. It wasn't so good at that time. At least now we don't have anything like that to put up with.

(*Ken F., sergeant*)

– Now the island isn't ours I feel very much like a second-class citizen being back here at the invitation of the UN. That isn't proper soldiering to me. I'm not saying I'd like a war to break out or anything of that sort, but I do find it dull poncing around in a little light blue hat and not having to worry about people shooting at you or throwing things at you. You'll still get a kid stick his tongue out at you in the street sometimes, but I don't know that he even knows you're British.

(*Eddie B., captain*)

– The thing was you see, when I was here before you felt people didn't appreciate you. The people back at home I mean: they had no real idea what all that business was about, and I don't think we had ourselves either really. I was quite shocked the next time I was back in Cyprus after we'd given them their independence, and I saw their national memorial which is statues of people coming out of prison into the sunlight to freedom. That's the way the Cypriots look at it, and it's not all that wonderful a feeling to know that's how people think of you now.

(*Roger A., major*)

– I could get home on leave for £10 if I went on what they call one of those "indulgence flights". You can only get it if there's a spare seat: but if someone turns up at the last minute with a ticket, you're off. The snag is it costs £108 to come back, and you have to get your return ticket before they'll give you the indulgence.

(*Danny C., private*)

– I reckon it's harder on the wives and children back home who can't come out here to see their husbands. They have a picture of them spending all their time on the beaches sunbathing and lots of half-naked Swedish birds wandering around. You've seen it: but if you do happen to see one of them Swedish birds anywhere, make me the first one you tell eh?

(*Michael M., corporal*)

– I know they're having a smashing time out there, seeing somewhere different and being in a place like that where there's plenty of lovely sunshine, not like this wretched weather we're having here. From what I hear it's almost a holiday. He says he'll take me there himself one day . . . Well one day could be any day a long way ahead couldn't it? I've heard some of the officers' wives go out: it's all right for them, they've got the money and can afford it. I know there's nothing to stop us going, but you do have to think about the money all the time. He's sent me several photographs of him enjoying himself: about all you can do is grit your teeth and say well good on you.

(Madge D., lance corporal's wife)

— It's not a big deal for me, telling the kids at Christmas Daddy's lying on the beach in the sun in Cyprus. They'd sooner he was here and I'd sooner he was too. But in all honesty knowing Roger I'm sure he'd sooner be here with us and his family at Christmas time too.

(Linda V., private's wife)

iv. England

— When your husband comes back after he's been away on a six-months' unaccompanied, that's the make or break time. You have the first couple of weeks' honeymoon time, in bed together as much as you can as often as you can and all that sort of thing: but then you've got to get back down to the natural day-to-day living together business. You start noticing little things about each other you'd forgotten: the noises he makes when he's cleaning his teeth or on the loo: or he notices the way you blow your nose or burp or something. Either you like it or at least don't mind it, or it starts to grate: and if it does that then you are, you're really in trouble.

(Eileen R., corporal's wife)

— After a few days it starts coming, he says "I hear you and Jean were seeing a lot of each other while I was away" and you say "Yes that's right she was terrific, I don't know what I'd have done without her." When it gets hard is when it starts to be "Did you have a lot of trouble with the washing machine then?" And you think "What's he on about?" And what he's on about is that some kind soul's told him the plumber was round a lot.

(Doreen G., private's wife)

– What it all comes down to to my mind is trust. If you don't trust each other, trust each other completely and not be asking niggling questions all the time, then you might as well forget the whole thing, it'll never work and it'll go on getting worse.

(Margaret B., sergeant's wife)

– Last year we had, for the average soldier, between 100 and 165 days' separation from his wife or his wife and family. This year so far we shall have – and this is only including the things we know about, the exercises that are already laid on – this year we shall have between 200 and 220 days. There's six months' unaccompanied, which is 180 days for a start, then all the rest. That's a hell of a lot, you know.

(Harold T., commanding officer)

– I think being in England's a right drag. It's not I don't like my wife and kids and home and all that, it's just so fucking boring.

(Ken T., private)

– I'd say I'm a bit disappointed with Army life in England. There's a lot of being mucked about, nothing happens and I don't think anything we do is very interesting. Practices for parades and Freedom Marches and all that, that's not really what I joined the Army for. After going to Belize for my first posting, where it was all new and different, after that coming back here is very boring. They said "Join the Army and see the world." Well the only two places I've seen so far is Belize and Colchester. There must be more world than that.

(Cliff E., private)

– Coming back to England after Cyprus's made me feel I'm definitely going to get out. I don't like being mucked around, doing stupid things, practising for parades and all that rubbish and all for poor money. So if I can get out I might go with Securicor or something of that sort. I think you feel it more in England that you don't get paid anything for overtime: you're on duty twenty-four hours, or on call for duty, and it doesn't matter whether you work

Saturday, Sunday, Christmas Day, Boxing Day or whatever, you'll not get no more money for it.

(*Fred J., lance corporal*)

— My main job recently was practising opening a car door. It was for the visit of the Queen Mother that we had. I was the one chosen to open the door of her car for her when she arrived on the parade ground, and hold it open while she stepped out. Then when the parade was over, I had to nip to the car when it arrived and whip the door open for her, timing it exactly as she stepped towards it. Then when I was sure she was safely tucked inside, I had to shut the door firmly: make sure it was really closed, but on the other hand not give it such a wallop she shot up in the air off her seat. Then I had to turn round and run like buggery across the parade ground down the alley at the back and round to the front door of the officers' mess. I had to train for that, it was timed with a stop-watch: because I had to get there before she arrived there in the car. I had to be standing stiff and upright and not be out of breath. Then when the car pulled up I had to step forward and open the door for her to get out. I don't mind telling you, it got fucking complicated at times, I thought I'd never get the hang of it. Practise practise practise, I was opening fucking car doors and shutting them in my sleep. I reckon I must be the best car door opener and shutter in the battalion but I don't expect I'll get no medal for it.

(*Les M., private*)

— I go home every night except when I'm on duty, my Mum and Dad only lives ten minutes away. Sometimes I have to get up in the morning at five o'clock, but most times I don't have to be in here at barracks till a quarter past eight. It's cheaper living at home than it is living in camp. But you only get one chance at being late: if you do it a second time you're on a charge. It's no good ringing up and saying your car's broken down, they won't accept that as an excuse for being late.

(*Jack D., lance corporal*)

— My wife and me have got this quarter now, and with the kiddy coming along that's nice. But it's not going to be easy to manage financially: in England you don't have any of the extra allowances you get overseas. We're not really saving any money: and we get a rent rebate, because if it wasn't for that we couldn't manage to have the quarter. We reckon to go out once a month, just the once, that's all, to a pub or a disco. We have to have a babysitter and pay her so it comes expensive. There's never any question of splashing out on my birthday or the wife's. All the furniture you can see is on the HP. I'd say we have about enough to live on but only just.

(Jim S., private)

— I think most people have the completely wrong impression. When I tell them my husband's got to be available twenty-four hours a day, 365 days a year, they don't believe it. But it's true and I think the pay for it is poor. We get knocks at the door at six o'clock in the morning, we've had our fair share. I mean at least when he's away I know I'm not going to have anyone coming round in that sort of way. But life's generally not easy. People don't realize there are privates on rent rebates, or if they've got kids on Family Income Supplements. We go out only rarely.

(Ann S., private's wife)

— It'll be better when we go abroad again: if it's an unaccompanied tour I could save up a bit of money, I'd send it home and the wife could put it in the bank.

(Arthur M., private)

— The main offence here is going absent without leave. There's more of it in England than you get abroad. If you're going to go home and have a break or if you're going to go off with a bird somewhere, there's not much point in getting done for one day absent so you make it worthwhile – a week or a fortnight, or in some cases several weeks. I think there's more temptation to go absent in England, because you've got more choices of places you can go.

(Peter G., private)

— We're not in any danger to speak of and we can go where we like and do what we like within limits. A few of the lads tend to spend their evenings drinking in pubs and fighting: on the whole they fight one another, and they give all soldiers a bad name as a result. I don't know that any of the local birds make a point of trying to get to know you here, like they do in other places. You go to Germany or Ireland and to girls there there's something different about a British soldier because they don't see all that many. But local people here in England, they think "Oh Christ a soldier, I don't want nothing to do with him."

(Bernard B., corporal)

– I've been in no trouble here so far. Well p'raps I'd better say I've not been caught for no trouble so far. But then I haven't done anything very much, except a bit of drinking and driving, a bit of fighting and frightening, and a bit of smoking.

(*Billy The Kid, private*)

– A bit of a problem is that there are certain pubs where soldiers aren't welcome, p'raps they've had trouble with them in the past. They can spot a soldier a mile off. I've more than once been with the wife and the landlord has looked at me and asked me to go somewhere else when I've gone up to the bar to order a drink. My wife doesn't like it when we go in pubs where there are soldiers, because she's always frightened something is going to start. In abroad countries they're usually glad to take your money: but here what they're thinking of mainly is their other customers and they might lose their licence.

(*Don J., sergeant*)

– It's an ideal life here, and I'm taking absolutely full advantage of it. At weekends I go sailing and fishing or I go up to London and stay with friends. I go to the theatre, opera, concerts, discos, take in all the new films and enjoy life to the full. I'm not saying I don't enjoy life to the full when we're not in England because I do: but I am saying that being an officer at what one might call one's home barracks is really exceedingly pleasant. Life at the moment is all good news. But I'm aware all the time that maybe this time today six months from now I'll be walking down a street in Belfast waiting for someone to take a crack at me.

(*Ian G., lieutenant*)

– On weekend leaves I tend to plunge into social life, anything to get away from the ghastly living here in the officers' mess. I have a girlfriend up in London, well not really a proper girlfriend, just someone I use for going to bed with and take to parties because she's a looker. We go out and have meals, look around the shopping piazza in Covent Garden, that sort of thing. I leave it to her to fix up parties for us to go to with her Chelsea and Kensington friends. I find it's an advantage with the birds to drop the word you're an Army officer: it'll get you into bed with more or less anyone you want. I think they like the suggestion of the rough tough battle-scarred fighter and that sort of thing. It's definitely a social asset to be able to say you're an officer.

(Lionel H., second lieutenant)

– This officers' mess here, while we've got the chance in England I think there should be more living out. Young subalterns for instance, three or four of them might be given a quarter and look after it themselves. The sort of life they lead in the mess with servants to bring them coffee and meals, a wine waiter in the evening and all the rest of it, life really isn't like that. I think they ought to be pushed out into society and given an opportunity to look after themselves: cook for themselves, learn budgeting and house management. Living like they do here in a very privileged world's not a situation I think should be encouraged.

(Edward N., captain)

– I think it's the indecisiveness of the civilians that I can't stand. I say to a girl "Where would you like to go this evening, what would you like to do?" and then I wait for her response. I know exactly what it's going to be. She says "Well, what would you like to do?" Sometimes I find it very difficult to keep my temper. I want to say to her "Look I've just asked you what you want to do, so for Christ's sake say what you want to do. I don't want to have a discussion about it. Make your mind up, say it, and we'll do it."

(Robert W., lieutenant)

– We had this Ladies Night in the mess and Marjorie turned up in a complete dinner-jacket outfit she'd hired at Moss Bros. The full fig: starched shirt, black tie, dinner-jacket, cummerbund, everything. I did admire her, she looked really dinky: all the other fellows commented about it the following day. I felt enormously proud, my girl had been the star of the evening.

(Adrian T., second lieutenant)

– Don't quote me about this in a way that I could be identified, but it's when we're here in barracks in England I start having big doubts about whether I really want to go for a commission or not. We call them "Ruperts", those young officers: and when you see the way they behave, or at least some of them do, in the mess, you think to yourself "I don't know that I want to mix in with that lot."

(George B., sergeant major)

– One of the difficulties in England is there are no yardsticks you can measure achievements by. In Ireland you count the number of terrorists arrested, weapons and explosives found and so on. But here there's no real measure of what you're achieving in terms of efficiency on exercises. I talk to the whole battalion as often as I can, about what we've achieved in the last few months, what we shall be doing in the next few. You get a few mumbles and groans when you say we shall be away for a week in August on exercises and so on: but at least you're not springing it on them, it keeps them in the picture. But it's hard for me to get feedback. I constantly have to ask people like my driver or my batman to tell me what the other ranks are feeling, and to tell me honestly so I can get a sense of the level of morale. But no one's going to volunteer because they think it's not their place to offer criticism to me.

(Mark D., commanding officer)

– Some people, especially civilians, will talk to you about us "playing war games", by which they're usually referring to exercises, but I think there are two things about exercises which they don't understand. We make them as realistic as we can, and the reason for it is this: we have to try and get everyone used to real battle conditions and they find themselves facing situations which they could very well encounter when they're fighting for real. We don't give them any reason for pretending it's all a game, quite the contrary. They have to wear battle gear all the time, they have to carry their packs, carry their rifles, dig in in trenches, sleep out in the rain and all the other things that might happen to them – so that if they did, they wouldn't be totally green and inexperienced. We impress upon them this is the real thing, and all the rules and restrictions of genuine battle apply. That's one side of it. The other one is equally important, and it's that if they were in a real battle, they should face it with something approaching the feeling that it's only an exercise. They should know in the heat of the moment exactly what to do and exactly how to react, because that's exactly how they've been trained. We don't want people suddenly overcome with a sense of "My God, this time it's for real." So we try to make it "for real" in the exercise as much as we can.

(Mark D., commanding officer)

– I think our exercises are not as realistic as they should be. When you think that racing drivers, yachtsmen and various others like that take really quite severe risks in practice, so that when the real time comes they'll be ready for it, and soldiers don't – well that's unrealistic. The thing I'm talking about in the main is live ammunition. I believe the Russians actually use it, they accept quite high casualty rates. I'm not suggesting we should go as far as they do but I think we could up the ante a little bit.

(*Tony J., lieutenant*)

– It seems mad to me, all the restrictions on exercises. We can't do certain things at certain times of the night because we get complaints from the civilians saying we're keeping them awake. They don't like convoys rumbling through their village in the early hours of the morning. We did a mock attack recently on an airfield, you should have seen the letters that came in. The local paper was full of complaints too. I don't know what they think, do they think if there's a war it'll be fought during the daytime at hours to suit them? That's when you really feel you're not appreciated by your own people in your own country. I think you should bring National Service back to give more people more idea of what it's really all about. On the other hand I think you should do away with the Freedom Marches, where we exercise our right to parade through a town. It's a lot of work and preparation, and in the end all it amounts to is drill. To my mind it's got fuck all to do with soldiering, whether you can keep in step with everybody else or not.

(*Barry E., private*)

– At the moment recruiting's very good, and we can pick and choose a bit. In fact we're getting to the stage when before long we shall have a waiting list, we'll almost be asking for three or four GCEs.

(*Don J., sergeant*)

– In my day no one really wanted to be in the Army: that was when we had National Service. Now the problem is with those who come in, they've volunteered and the cleverer ones want to get on, they want promotion as soon as they can. A single young man will get a good wage, working clothes, medical attention, accommodation, cheap food and all the rest of it. It's not a bad life for him. The problem comes when you get married and have a partly furnished house at about the same rent you pay for a council house. Because of the improved living conditions in society in general, we're getting HP problems for three-piece suites, colour tellies, videos and all the other status symbols. Then they start complaining about having to turn out early in the morning occasionally, or going away on exercises too much. There's no satisfying some people. And the real deadbeats are looking to get away by about four thirty every afternoon: I mean Jesus Christ.

(Norman M., sergeant major)

—When I was in the recruiting office the system we worked on with applicants, the young chaps who came there and said they wanted to join the Army, was we first of all gave them a basic intelligence test, and on the results of that we graded them 1, 2, 3, 4 and 5. If you were 4 or 5 you were too thick even to be a soldier: you couldn't learn anything or assimilate anything, so you were rejected. That left us with the 1s, 2s and 3s. We didn't take too many of the 1s. Even though the tests were very basic and anyone who passed as a 1 wasn't exactly a genius, even so they were the sort who were possibly going to question and argue too much and could perhaps gee-up the others into giving trouble. So although we had a few of the 1s – we called them "sparklers" by the way – we only had a leavening of them as you might say. We liked best the 2s and 3s: most of all the 3s, they were what you'd call ideal other-ranks material.

(Arthur W., major)

12 A Totally Different Country

— I was shit scared when I first come to Northern Ireland. Like everyone else. If someone says they're not, don't believe them. The feeling lasts about two weeks.

(*Len B., private*)

— We're here for two years. The first six months is exciting, the second six months is interesting, the third six months is boring. During the fourth six months your nerves are jangling. You think "How long is my luck going to hold out?"

(*David M., captain*)

— Ireland's nothing to be scared of if you look at it the right way. It gives you a chance to be a proper soldier. Provided you're switched on, you can reduce the danger to yourself by 90 per cent. The other 10 per cent you need luck for: because if the terrorists want to hit you they're going to try, and it's in the lap of the gods whether they'll succeed. So you've got to keep up your skills and work to keep yourself sharp. You've got to be constantly on the look out for the little details, like for instance a broken street lamp. Has it been smashed deliberately so as to make a dark area there when night falls? If that's a danger you report it straight away and try and get it repaired. Or a parked car will appear on a street where it wasn't there an hour before. You ask for a trace on it, find out who it belongs to and why it's there.

(*Reg D., sergeant*)

– The first week I come here I didn't like it. I was only nineteen and I'd not been nowhere else. When they told me I'd got to go out on the streets I was really scared. And the very first day I went out there was shooting: I don't think it was at us but it was nearer than I'd been in all my life to live ammunition being aimed in my direction. I was very jumpy. But you can't show it in front of your mates.

(*Ken J., private*)

– The main thing I notice is that it's made me swear a lot. I never used to swear at all, but being here in Londonderry it's all the time fucking this and shit that. On and on all the time. Everybody does it, and you somehow feel you're going to be unlucky if you try to make yourself different. What a fucking place this is eh? I'm a different person, it has, it's completely changed my whole fucking life.

(*Dick H., lance corporal*)

– As soon as I arrived I was given a briefing, then I was sent out on a night patrol with a very experienced sergeant. I immediately noticed how vulnerable we were as we walked along the street: both from the side streets coming down into the main one, and from the gaps between the houses. I was told to operate one brick – that's four men – and take them down a street. I did it very slowly and gingerly I can tell you. It wasn't so much I was worried about getting shot myself, but what would happen if one of them did, on the very first occasion I was in charge. I don't know how they must have felt: they were all much more experienced than I was, but their safety had been put in my hands.

(*Jonathan P., second lieutenant*)

– This is my first posting. They told me when I got here I'd get lots of training. What they didn't tell me was what they meant by training was patrolling the streets so people could take pot shots at you. The first time it happened, the corporal in our brick said to me "Right son, now you're getting the idea." So far we've never fired back. At least you can say it isn't boring, it makes you feel you're a soldier.

(*Bill L., private*)

– When we arrived it was a bit scary, but that only lasted a day and a night. Now I've got used to it: rushing into houses, kicking down the door, searching them, I like all that. We had a couple of grenades thrown at us last week and one or two shots, but no one got hurt. I think it's dead good. We've arrested a few people on the streets as well: I don't go mad about it, but I like doing it, it seems to me it's proper soldiering.

(*Mick K., private*)

– I've only just come to Londonderry and I think it really is, it's a really shitty job like sewer cleaning. I think about my own home town, and try to imagine myself going round with a platoon in the streets at night, knocking on the doors of people's houses and demanding to be let in to search them. I can't imagine doing that with people in my own home town, I can't imagine living in my own home town and people coming and doing that to us. I reckon it's a pretty shitty job, I really do.

(*Paul K., second lieutenant*)

– My first experience of a riot, I was back man this side in a brick. We were going down the street and someone threw a glass bomb, you know a milk bottle with petrol in it. I dived behind the wall of a front garden, but the sergeant came up behind me. "Get up you bastard," he shouted and he gave me a kick up the arse. It hurt, but it got me up.

(*Teddy M., private*)

– I always try to remember that the majority of the population are not people who would shoot you, or people who would wish you to be shot at.

(*Ron P., lance corporal*)

– The first time I came here I saw it all very clear cut. But not now. I don't like trying to explain to an eighteen-year-old lad who's just joined that he's a target for people to shoot at, because he's supposed to be a buffer between two sets of people. Soldiers are just the tools of politicians.

(*Bert M., sergeant*)

– We've got several of these little fortified posts scattered around the city. This one is the worst. As you can see, three rooms for thirty men to live and sleep and eat in, all at the same time. Bunks pulled up together, all the cooking done in that corner on the table there, two TV sets showing videos all the time, patrols coming in or going out, people talking, others playing cards, others trying to sleep. It's like a circus.

(*Peter D., lance corporal*)

– I like it better over the other side of the river. Ten days here in this
fort, it drives you up the fucking wall. All grotty and gungy, I mean
look for yourself. There's three of us got fleas, and everyone's using
the same blankets. And you're going in lousy houses all the time,
and don't know what you're going to bring back. It drives you
barmy.

(*Eddie C., lance corporal*)

– Living where we are, in a tiny fortress like this, all of you crammed
in one room, high walls and barbed wire all round the outside of it,
you learn a lot about the thirty people you're with. You can only go
out of the gate on patrol, into the ops room, into your bunk or
watch the telly. You learn most about yourself. That after ten days
you stink, mentally and physically.

(*Andrew J., second lieutenant*)

– When you're on look out duty in the sangar at the end it gets
boring and that's when it's dangerous. You're staring through these
binoculars all the time, at the stones, the walls, the streets down
there: and watching over there for stolen cars. You're supposed to
keep the list of numbers in your head, but your mind goes dull. You
go off duty three hours and have a bit of sleep, then you're back on
stag again for another four and a half hours – one hour and a half in
the sangar here, another one and a half hours along the wall there,
then another one and a half hours further along at the end. Makes
you dizzy.

(*Sam W., private*)

– Here, the bad times are the good times, and hard times are the best
times. When you're in a place like this in an area like this where
there's likely to be trouble, you only get about three hours' un-
broken sleep ever. There's danger, life's rough, the conditions
you're living in are awful – I really enjoy all that. I said to my wife
"You can't imagine what it's like" and she said "No I can't.
Someone said to me the other day they felt sorry for you. I told them
not to, I said you were having a terrific time." She was right.

(*Fred S., sergeant major*)

– We came out of this alley and standing right in front of us on the
pavement were two men. One of them, the only name we had for
him was "Cowboy": but there was no doubt who he was. We'd had
plenty of opportunity to study pictures of him, he'd been respon-

sible for several deaths and injuries. And there he was, just a few yards away. His friend looked at us, then at him, and then he started to run. He shouted "Run for it Cowboy, they won't shoot." So Cowboy turned and started to run. He'd taken about six steps when I gave the order to fire. Later on one of the lads pinned up a cartoon he'd drawn on the wall of the room by where they eat. Two men were running and a bubble coming out of one's mouth was saying, "Come on Cowboy, run, they won't shoot."

(*Eddie P., sergeant*)

– Now I'm all the time questioning what we're doing here: controlling the civilian population basically but I'm wondering whether there's any end in view. As I see it there's no solution in sight. We hear about "men of goodwill on both sides being given time to work it out". Well if you ask me, "men of goodwill" are getting fewer and fewer, and more and more disillusioned themselves.

(*Bob R., second lieutenant*)

– We're told we're buying time for the politicians, but we're not: there's no more time left to buy. Because of British politicians who're now dead, and what they did all those years ago to preserve their own self-esteem and power, innocent people are being killed all the time – soldiers who weren't even born then, and civilians the same. It's absolutely ludicrous. By the way, don't identify me on this.

(*Alan D., lieutenant*)

– The most exciting time on the streets was when I got shot at. I say I got shot at but it was our brick that was shot at. Everyone felt the same, really high: we was darting about the road and jumping into doorways to shelter, it was exciting like nothing else I've experienced before. At least you felt something was going on. When you start shooting back you go cold: at least I do, because that's how I've been trained, not to be excited when shooting.

(*Harry R., private*)

– When I go out I'm in charge of two bricks – that's two four-man patrols, sometimes one or two more. We move along the streets in fours, a man at each corner: like yesterday when you were with us, two at the front at each corner, two at the back also at each corner. I

enjoy it. I'd be happy to stay doing it: I think I could really get into it
in a big way. But you can become over-involved.

(*Bob L., second lieutenant*)

— When you're shot at you automatically do what you're trained to
do, which is dive for the nearest cover. Then you lift your head
carefully with your rifle at the ready to shoot back if necessary. It's a
sort of automatic response, you don't have time to feel frightened or
anything. That only comes afterwards: you look back on it and you
think "Christ, I'd never have heard that shot if it had hit me."

(*Leonard A., private*)

— I like the challenge of the threat to us when we're on the streets on
patrol. It's me and my team against them, us against the terrorists.
They're trying to kill us, we're trying to capture or if necessary kill
them. It's good.

(*David F., second lieutenant*)

— The best thing about it is being with your mates. I know that
sounds corny but it's true. It's always the same four of you in the
brick. You're all frightened together, you know they've all got the
same feeling when you're out on the street as you have. You know
there's an M60 around, that's an automatic rifle like a machine gun,
and it's looking for a soldier. Maybe it's pointing at you or one of
your lot, but you won't know where it is till it starts up. So you're all
waiting to hear it. You're looking down the street, at the houses, at
the roofs, and trying not to think too much about it. But you think
"Well if it's going to get us it's going to get us!"

(*Bill H., private*)

— You're trained to ignore street abuse. A violent action, you react
with something short sharp and brutal, but words you ignore. Now
and again someone'll take a punch at you in a mix-up, and I've
taken a swipe back. But you've got to remember your nearest help is
maybe twenty minutes away. There's only thirty of you in the
platoon, and you're facing a crowd of about three or four hundred.
So you've got to think very hard before you let it get to violence. If
no one is injured or killed then afterwards you can claim it as a
success. But when they start throwing bricks and petrol bombs you
know you can't retreat. You have to start to move forward because
you can't let anyone drive you back.

(*Eric N., lieutenant*)

— I was involved trying to break up a riot, and I caught a brick which cut open the side of my face. That made me only walking wounded, so it was a bit before I was taken to hospital. When I got to the casualty department there was this long queue of about twenty to thirty people. Half of them were people I'd just been in among in the riot on the street, and there were three other soldiers in uniform besides myself. We were dotted here and there in the queue waiting to have our injuries attended to, along with the fucking rioters who'd caused them in the first place, they were having their injuries attended to that our lads had caused. It was a funny scene.

(*Benny M., private*)

— It gives you a scary feeling if you're patrolling the street when a man passes you who you know's involved with the terrorists. Your officers might not know him that well: or they might be letting him walk around so they can keep an eye on him and see where he goes. I didn't like it when someone did what they did last week. He said "Hello Dick" to me, just to let me know he knew my name and who I was. Nobody could object to someone passing the time of day with you like he did: only it didn't mean what it sounded as though it meant.

(*Dick N., corporal*)

— On the streets you have to use a tough action, a physical action if necessary to prevent yourself and your men being killed. We've calculated that when someone appears unexpectedly on a street corner in front of you, you have slightly under three seconds in which to decide if it's a gunman, and whether or not you should raise your rifle, aim, and fire. If you make the wrong decision, either you've had it or the other person has. Neither of those alternatives is very pleasant to think about.

(*Larry M., sergeant*)

— They say when you see a brick coming towards you, you jump up in the air and nut it. That way you get yourself £40. When somebody's been injured, his mates talk as if the only thing they were interested in was how much compensation he was going to get. I had a discussion with three of them last week: one of their mates had had one of his fingers smashed and it was going to have to be amputated. One said to me "Is it true sir, he's going to get ten thousand pounds for that because it's the index finger of his right hand?" I said "I'm not the one who decides, I've no idea what he'll get." Then one of the others said "I say it'll be nearer five hundred pounds than ten thousand pounds." The third one said "We're having a sweep. Would you like to join in sir, it's a fiver a guess?" I suppose that's the right way for them to take it.

(*David D., captain*)

– In the last few months I've found I can be much harder than I thought I could be as an officer on the street, splitting up groups of people who are shouting at each other. A couple of weeks ago one of my blokes got hit by a civilian, and naturally he punched the other guy back. All the civilians on the street gathered round, they were very angry and it looked as though a nasty situation was going to blow up. I went over and I said to some "You go over on to that pavement" and to others "And you go over there on the opposite pavement." I got them all separated, then went in the middle of the street with my men and said to both groups loudly and clearly "We're staying here until you disperse back to your homes." I was astonished that that's exactly what they did. Afterwards when I came back to barracks here off duty, the first thing I did was go in the mess bar and have a large whisky. My hands were trembling, and I was trying to stop anyone else seeing it. I couldn't get out of my mind that maybe fifty or sixty grown-up people had done what I told them to. I'm only twenty-one and if they'd decided not to do what I said I've no idea what would have happened. Why did they do it? It's amazing.

(*Trevor S., second lieutenant*)

– Unfortunately I can only react, I can't initiate. Even in the dark we stand out like sore thumbs in our uniform. The terrorist can and does wear civilian clothes, coats with collars turned up, anoraks, and in his appearance there's nothing different about him to the ordinary civilian.

(*Tim G., lieutenant*)

– There'll be a cataclysm involving tremendous bloodshed, I think it's inevitable. But the time has come, it's past, for us to stop pretending we can be amiable policemen and hold the ring.

We're trying to stop the flow of history because we backed the wrong side in 1922. We're here in a peace-keeping role and we're constrained quite rightly by the politicians. But if after all these years we're still losing lives and getting nowhere, then my personal feeling's one of bitter despair.

(*James L., second lieutenant*)

– Why are we here? I ask myself all the time, and it's the subject we all talk about every night pretty near in the mess. Kids throwing stones at you because you're in uniform, four of you facing two hundred people yelling and shouting – and this is all due to different governments' continual policy or lack of it. You think "Shit, I don't want to be here doing this, I don't want to be giving orders to these men to stand firm and take all the abuse and the things that are thrown at them."

(*Eddie P., sergeant*)

– On the streets when people and kids are stoning soldiers and you've got to give the order to fire baton rounds, you know they're not accurate and you know the kids could get hit. OK so they shouldn't be there in the first place, and as a soldier you're trained to fire and give orders to fire when it's necessary, and minimum use of force and all that. Well I don't like it, I hate it, but that's what I'm trained to do. And last time I was in Northern Ireland one of my closest friends got shot and killed and that does something to you, makes you bitter and full of violent feelings towards everyone. That's something which as a soldier you've got to control. If you didn't and couldn't then the only logical thing for you would be to get out of the Army.

(*Chris J., major*)

– I've never seen so much hate in all my life as I've seen in Londonderry. The dreadful thing is that they're religious things that are driving people apart, and I just can't understand that. You see four-year-olds out on the street at midnight or past and you think "My God, that's terrible." And then you go to the Creggan or Bogside and you find little council houses where they've got eight or ten children, and they have to sleep in the beds on a rota system.

(*Derek T., corporal*)

– We've done a few searches, what we call "rummage searches". Four houses next to each other in a terrace, we go in to keep them on the hop. We usually carry them out about an hour before dawn. The purpose is to make sure they know it isn't safe to hide explosives or weapons for the men. Every step you take you keep your eyes peeled. Because once they know you're in the area, they know where to find you if they decide they want to come after you.

(*Patrick K., lance corporal*)

– We have two vehicles and ten soldiers. Two drivers stay with the vehicles, two soldiers go round the back gardens in case anyone comes running out, and the rest come with me to the front door. We knock, then we go in: by that I mean we knock and then we kick the door down. You have to remember the man or men we're looking for are armed, and won't hesitate to start shooting if they're there.

(*Len F., sergeant*)

– We did a search this morning. It was the house of a woman with five children, we went in about five thirty. Four of her kids had got measles and we had to tell her to get them all up. We didn't wreck the house, but we turned it over properly, we did our job thoroughly. Her husband is a wanted man, and of course we didn't expect to find him there but we thought we might get some ammunition, or evidence he'd been there. On the whole she took it very well: she wasn't very pleased, but she didn't say much, just gave us dirty looks. I mean eight soldiers clumping round her house, and her and the kids standing there in their night clothes in the dark early hours getting cold. I'm surprised she didn't make more fuss: but perhaps she's getting used to it, after all this is the thirteenth time she's had her house searched in three weeks. We had an address, a time to go in, and the name of who we were looking for and all the rest of it. It's a job and we did it.

(*Kevin J., corporal*)

– It's tricky if you do find a load of explosives or rifles, because you feel you want to get violent about it. These people have been all nice to you and yet they're hiding guns or maybe hiding people who'd kill you. Whatever they say, they'd help someone kill you. You think "I never want to see any of you fuckers again." And then there you are a couple of days later, they're all pleasant and nice and talking to you on the street.

(*Harry G., corporal*)

– I think Northern Ireland is one of the loveliest countries I've ever been to in my whole life. My wife and children are in a very nice quarter well outside the city. We've become friends with a local man and his wife, and my wife and I sometimes go to their house for meals. They take us out at weekends in their car to show us the other side of Northern Ireland, to get us away from the city and let us see what a beautiful country they have. They're very proud of it, they've every reason to be.

(Tom S., sergeant)

– The incident occurred when we were on our way across the city in a car in plain clothes. My mate Eddie was driving and we gave two others a lift. We dropped them off where they wanted to be, then we started off for where we were heading. Eddie drove down the hill to a crossroads: there were traffic lights and they were against us. I remember it all quite clearly, it still runs through my mind like a film. There was a big red car in front of us. When the lights changed we expected it to move but it didn't. From the pavement side nearest where I was two men with pistols stepped out of a shop doorway, then a man with an automatic weapon came round the other side and started to fire. The red car moved, Eddie slammed his foot on the accelerator and we shot across the road hitting some railings, so I knew then he'd been injured. The men with the pistols had run across the crossroads after us. I felt one bullet go in my hand, and I knew another had hit me but I didn't know where. I didn't know that altogether I'd got five bullets in me. I jerked open the car door and rolled out, then got up and started to run up the street. There was a graveyard on the opposite side of the road, and I somehow remember thinking if I was going to die the thing to do would be to go in the graveyard and die there. I tried to make for it but I fell over between some traffic bollards in the middle of the road. Then I staggered back on to the pavement and there were some small houses with their front doors on the street. One of them opened, and a big woman grabbed hold of me. She said "Come on son, I won't let the fucking Brits get you." I started to scream at her, I said "You fucking cow, take your fucking hands off me" and she slammed the door shut. I don't know where it'd come from but then an armoured carrier pulled up next to me. A soldier stuck his head out and he said "What's wrong, is something the matter?" I said "What do you think you stupid fucker." My language was, it was dreadful. A lot of soldiers jumped out and dragged me into the vehicle and they got me to the hospital a few minutes away. I was finding it hard to breathe then, because I'd got four bullets in my chest. The nurses and doctors were trying to get my clothes cut off so they could give me an injection, and I was screaming and swearing at them and telling them to leave me alone. I heard one of the soldiers say my mate was dead, he'd been shot through the head. Then I was moved to a military hospital. I'd no idea who the men were who shot me, but I was moved because they might have come in to finish me off when they heard I was still alive, because for all they knew I might have recognized them. I was in hospital two and a half months.

My fiancée was a local Irish girl I'd met. A Catholic. We're married now.

(*Ken D., corporal*)

– The last time I went home I was walking down the street with my Mum going shopping. You can't stop looking everywhere: your eyes are looking up to the rooftops, every time you're approaching a corner your step slows down a little bit. She asked me what was the matter but I couldn't explain it. It's not exactly nerves, it's the feeling you get you'd better never stay still and give somebody a free shot at you.

(*Harry R., private*)

– When I went back on leave, the first day I went out shopping with my sister we were walking down the street and a car came past and backfired. Before I knew what I was doing I'd jumped over a garden wall and was crouching down behind it. My sister burst into tears. She said it was horrible to see me like that.

(*Ken J., private*)

– We'd been called out on a report of a bomb in a factory, we were sent to clear the area. We got everyone out but it was a set-up, there was a sniper waiting. All I remember with any clarity is the look on the face of the soldier standing next to me by our patrol car. A look of horror, he could see I'd been shot, he was aware of it before I was. I was wearing my flak jacket but the bullet got in round my back here. I don't know for certain who shot me, I can only guess, I was told he was seventeen at the time. I've met him since, I've seen him on the street. I don't know if he knows it was me he shot, to him it was probably simply a soldier in uniform. When I recovered, the next time I was on the streets there was rioting and I felt angry: not because of what had happened to me, but because one of my friends had been killed the day before. I was very tempted to tell my men to start firing because of personal anger, but I didn't.

When I was in hospital I was overwhelmed by the number of cards and flowers sent to me by the people at the factory. And school kids wrote me letters and said they hoped I'd get better soon.

(Jeremy C., captain)

– When I knew I was a soldier was one day I was out in a Land Rover. We slowed down to avoid some parked cars, and someone threw a nail bomb in the back. That sort of thing stops you with a jolt: you suddenly realize it isn't exciting, it's bloody horrible. None of my men were killed, but several were severely injured. It makes you realize you're in a different country physically and mentally.

(Geoff H., corporal)

– One of my soldiers was injured and his parents came over to visit him in hospital. On the drive back to the airport when they were on their way home, the man's father wanted to talk: one of the things he mentioned with considerable irony was that he'd been with SOE in France in the war. He said the skills and techniques and dedication which he used there were exactly the same as those being used by the terrorists here now that had caused the near-killing of his son.

(Frank N., captain)

– What you have to understand is that we're the good guys. You have to understand that, I have to understand that: we're the good guys. The terrorists are not freedom fighters or men with ideals resorting to violence because they can't think what else to do: they're the bad guys. We're the good ones, and they're the bad ones, and if we don't believe that we're lost.

(Roger F., lieutenant)

– Last week I had to write to the parents of one of my lads and tell them he'd been killed. I told them he was a soldier, he died for his country, and he died in a most honourable situation as a member of a peace-keeping force, doing his best for all the people of this country. But I don't know what I'm supposed to say in letters like that, what I'm supposed to write. We all know there's no solution to this fucking problem and the best thing we can do is go away.

(Eric C., major)

– I mean what are we doing here? The Northern Irish are saying
"Never" to the unification of Ireland: and if they mean that, then
the way I see it is that we've either got to stay here for ever, or we've
got to withdraw and let them sort it out. The mistake was made in
the 1920s when they decided on partition. For ever afterwards
there've been only the shouts by the Ulstermen, "No compromise"
"No surrender" and all the rest of it. It seems to me we're left in the
middle to take the brickbats.

(*Harry N., sergeant*)

– There's lots of pubs we're not supposed to go in. The Army are
very good, as soon as you arrive they give you a list of all the places
that are off limits. My mates and me make a point of going into
them as soon as we can, to see what it is about them that makes them
out of bounds. I've been in every single one, I've got the list here and
you can see they're all ticked off. I think it's very good of the Army to
make it so easy for us.

(*Len K., private*)

– We go wherever we go together: the places we're supposed to go,
the places we're not supposed to go. There's a disco up the road
called The Roof: me and Trevor are in there whenever we get the
chance. If we was caught we'd be shot: not by the terrorists, by the
Army.

(*Donald T., private*)

– There's lots of places are out of bounds to us troops here, and I
never go nowhere that's out of bounds because my wife made me
promise it. She's a local girl, we got married a few weeks ago, we
met at a disco. She lives in a quarter with me: before that she was
living on the Bogside estate and working in a factory the other side
of the river. She didn't let on about me, it would have been more
than her life was worth. Any girl who goes out with a British soldier
gets called "Soldier's dolly", "Brit lover" and a few other things I
won't say.

(*Terry J., private*)

– There's a lady up the street, we call her Mum, she'll give us a cup of
tea any time we like. She gave us a Christmas party and got a lot of
the girls in from the houses round about. It was weird, they was
Catholic and Protestant, and we was dancing with them all: you'd

be dancing with a Catholic girl, then a Protestant girl and you can't tell any difference between one and another.

(*Andy A., private*)

— I'm marrying a girl I've met here. She's a Protestant, but we think it would be wiser to have the wedding over in England and her to stay there a while until I go back and join her. We're both aware of the danger there is to her. I think it's more to her than to me if she were to stay here, so she's going to stay in England with my mother until I get there.

(*Reg F., lance corporal*)

— We met at a disco and we went out a few times, and after a bit she told me that she loved me and I told her I loved her, and it was true for both of us. So we had that much in common to start with, although she was a Catholic and me well I suppose I'm what's called a Protestant.

(*Keith H., private*)

— It takes great courage for a Catholic Irish girl even to talk to a Brit, let alone go out with him or marry him. Why they should want to is something I don't understand. You could say depending on your attitude that they were sensible girls or they were stupid girls. But it takes a bit of doing. If one of your men comes to you and says he's got this girl and he's going to marry her, you tend to think there must be something about her.

(*Stan P., sergeant major*)

— She's twenty-one, but even though I didn't have to I thought I ought to ask her Dad. I was in the barracks and you can't get permission to go over the river to the bad side at night. So I bunked off and hired a car and drove over. I think her Dad hadn't been keen on her marrying a Brit, but at least that made him see I was serious, so he gave his OK. But there was no question of it being a church wedding or of any of her family coming: she'd stepped right over the line about what's permitted to a Catholic.

(*Malcolm H., private*)

— When I was in hospital for my first baby, a nurse came and bent over me one evening and said in a whisper, "Is your husband a soldier?" I nodded my head, and she just gave me an understanding look and a nod and went off. There was a woman from the Creggan estate on the one side of me, and one from the Bogside on the other. After my baby was born they took me up from the labour ward and put me in a different room. There were three other women there, and it was three days before we all found out we were all married to soldiers.

(Wendy W., private's wife)

– You never know in Ireland if your husband's coming home or not. Every car that stops anywhere near the house, I wonder if it's someone coming to tell me something's happened to him. I've been here a year now, and I just can't get used to it. My sister's married to a soldier too, and he was badly shot and injured. It sounds a terrible thing to say but in a kind of way I feel it wouldn't be fair if my husband escaped.

(Betty E., private's wife)

– My husband was wounded on the streets, and it took them two hours to come up to the quarter on the estate where we were living and tell me. They'd been looking at a car and shots were fired and one of them hit Geoff in the stomach. I didn't go around crying because of the children: I told them their Dad was in hospital and he'd got a poorly tummy.

My mother-in-law thinks I should hate the person who did it, but you can't hate someone you don't know. They were aiming to shoot a soldier, not my husband in particular. The other thing I remind myself of is that he could have done the same thing himself, or worse: there could be an Irish woman somewhere, feeling the same thing about my husband as I do about hers.

(Sandra K., lance corporal's wife)

– When our second child was born I had a bad time in the hospital. She was born on the evening of Bloody Sunday, and there were two other women in the ward with me, one's brother had been killed by the British soldiers and the other one's father had been badly hurt. I couldn't tell them I was Irish and the wife of a British soldier, and the baby I'd had that day was the child of a British soldier. It was the worst time I ever had in my life. I asked one of the nurses in a whisper if she'd go and phone my husband and tell him we had a daughter. I said, "Only please tell him he's not to come here." She was a nice girl, she understood why: so my husband never came to the hospital to see me, he didn't see our baby until I took her home.

(Joan P., private's wife)

– When I met him he was at one of the fortified posts and I worked in a shop selling newspapers and tobacco opposite. There was a café next door to us, actually we met in there and started talking. I lived in the Creggan, I couldn't be seen regularly with a British soldier so we had to find somewhere to meet over the other side of the river. I'm Catholic, he's not, my parents weren't at all keen, I couldn't ever take him home. I told no one at work I was going out with a soldier and no one found out. We got married just before he came back to England, and I came over to England with him. Some of the English wives were a bit hostile to me at first: you could understand that, because their men were getting attacked on the streets in my area. I felt very lonely in England because I'd never been anywhere away from home before.

When we had our first baby, after a while I took her back when she was a few months old to see my Mam. My Dad'd died and she wrote me a letter saying she'd like to see us. I hadn't seen her then for five years, and when I came back there was a terrible atmosphere because of the Army doing house searches in the area. I expect my Mam had told people from round about I was coming back. The first night, about midnight after I'd gone to bed there was this terrible noise: a lot of them'd got together in the street outside and they were rattling their dustbin lids on the pavement, to let me know they knew I was there. I didn't know what was going to happen next, whether they'd break in or throw bricks through the window or what they were going to do, so I hid lying on the bedroom floor with my baby all night.

Next morning I said to my Mam "I can't stop here another minute." And so I went back to Belfast and caught the first plane home. When I got in the house my husband said "What are you doing here, I thought you'd taken Annie to see your Mam?" I said to him "I'm never going to see my Mam again." I haven't and she's sixty-nine and she's never been in an aeroplane in her life. She can't visit England so that's the end of it.

(*Helen B., corporal's wife*)

– I've sometimes thought if I'd been born in another country, I might well have been a guerilla, a terrorist, a revolutionary fighter or whatever. I'm sure if I'd been born in a Catholic area in Londonderry I could well be in the IRA. Fighting men have more in common with each other than those who send them to fight. I respect the dedication of the IRA. I don't like their uninhibited violence but this isn't to say I don't recognize some of them are

idealists, even those who use criminal methods may be partly
motivated by idealism.

(Steve E., major)

– He's sometimes said he enjoyed Northern Ireland more than
anywhere he'd ever been. Because he said all the time "The old
adrenalin was flowing." Enjoyed it! Christ, it was the most miserable time of my life: I was waiting to have a baby, it was absolutely
God-awful. I kept hearing snatches on the radio news at different
times of the day: and it always seemed to be Northern Ireland this, a
soldier was killed in Northern Ireland, Northern Ireland that, two
soldiers were killed in Northern Ireland today, on and on. Some
days I got nearly hysterical, I thought I'd go to Belfast and get the
next plane home, I just couldn't stand it. The best time in his life!
Jesus!

(Pamela M., captain's wife)

13   At the Edge of the Common

   i.   *Idiots without brains:*
        Andrew Nash, second lieutenant

  ii.   *Thinking the unthinkable:*
        Donald Morris, lieutenant

 iii.   *All those selfish bitches:*
        Susan Shaw, private's wife

  iv.   *Utterable contempt:*
        Jennifer Long, captain's wife

   v.   *And furthermore*

i.   Idiots without brains:
Andrew Nash, second lieutenant

– What else have we been doing since we last talked, oh yes I know, we've been at Greenham Common, I expect you'll be interested in that. It'd be more exciting if I had anything to tell you about it, but it all passed off without any incident. There were no riots, no ladies tried to climb the fence, we didn't massacre any civilians, so all in all we had a pretty quiet time.

There was a bit of a flap wasn't there, something said in Parliament about the soldiers being ready if necessary to shoot? That caused a great deal more stir than anything that actually happened, because as I've told you nothing happened. We were there to guard the perimeter, we were helping the police do their job which they hadn't enough manpower to do at that particular time. I don't know what they were expecting but I gather they had a tip-off about something. For all I know it may have been genuine, us being there may have stopped the women from trying something, but that's all conjecture.

What do I think of them? The women? Well obviously I think they're potty, idiots without brains every one of them. Why "obviously"? Well because I don't think they understand the situation this country's in. We're dependent on America for our survival in any future war, and if the Americans want bases here to fire cruise missiles from I honestly don't see any reason why they shouldn't have them. They're after all a deterrent, and their foreign policy and our foreign policy is based on the theory of deterrence. Whether you agree with it or not that's our foreign policy. Parliament – or anyway the part of it that forms the government – has decided in its wisdom we should have these missiles here as our contribution to

NATO strategy. It wouldn't make the faintest difference to the international situation between the USA and Russia if the missiles were here, in Ireland, in the Isles of Scilly or wherever. Our government has agreed to them being in the UK, and that's the sole and single point.

If the women at Greenham Common disagree strongly with them being here presumably they're not suggesting they should be somewhere else in the British Isles. The only way they're going to bring about the Americans withdrawing them . . . well that's something they haven't a cat in hell's chance of. The only people who can get the Americans to take their weapons away are our government. So the women to my mind should be squatting and demonstrating round the Houses of Parliament, not out in the Berkshire countryside. I don't feel they've thought the thing through at all.

When I was at university I met a lot of women, and a number of men too, who took up that same sort of stance. I found it very difficult to have any patience with them. We used to have arguments going on long into the night about this whole business of Russia and the West. It seemed to me some of them were out and out communists, because to them anything Russia did was OK and everything America did was wrong. There was no arguing with them, no discussing, no point of contact at all.

The others were the ones I called the "Foggy Thinkers". They had very little perception of the realities of the world: their attitude seemed to be that if you were nice to people, they'd be nice back to you. I was at university on secondment from the Army and I'd already seen service in Ireland. I knew bloody well the fallacy of that argument and I truly believed, as I still do now, that some people are . . . well, to put it in one word, evil. There's nothing they won't stop at to achieve the particular end they have in view. It was certainly true of the IRA terrorists: they'd kill their own people if they thought it made their opposition to the presence of the British troops clear. And I honestly believe the Russians equally would stop at nothing to achieve the world superiority for their ideas.

I used to argue with some of the more particularly intransigent girls but I made no more impression on them than they did on me. I won't say I saw any of them at Greenham I knew, but I did see many exactly like them. I've read about them in the newspapers, I've had the pamphlets pushed at me, I've seen their spokesmen – sorry, that's got to be spokespersons hasn't it – on television, and listened to them expounding their ideas. And still the simple fact of the matter is the Americans are not going to take their cruise missiles away. And far and away the largest majority of the British population don't want them to, because they know it's the only security we've got. I think these women have got caught up in some kind of vague ideology which is absolutely silly and unrealistic. It irritates me when they take up the attitude that we, soldiers, are being warlike in helping protect the base from them. We're not. We want peace in the world just as much as they do: but what we're doing, or helping to do in guarding the perimeter, is a far more sensible contribution to peace than the shouting and demonstrating they indulge in. That gets them nowhere, and it never will.

As a soldier it's part of my job to protect our society, whether from the Russians, the IRA, or from any other extremist group that wants to use violence and not hold free elections. The women may not like what our government's doing, but in that case they must get rid of the government in the proper manner and persuade the next government to tell the Americans to take the cruise missiles away. We're in the business of doing whatever we're told to by the government of the day. So long as our government continues to behave defensively in the world I'm happy to go along with my order.

And as a rider to all that, I'd like to add that a fair number of the Greenham women were extremely offensive in their speech and shouted obscenities at the soldiers and the police. The soldiers were not allowed to shout back, though I know a lot of them when they came off duty at the edge of the Common let fly once they got out of the women's hearing, and were just as coarse and vulgar about the women as the women had been about them.

ii.   Thinking the unthinkable:
Donald Morris, lieutenant

— Quite a lot of the men when we got to Greenham were in something of a spin, particularly the younger officers. I don't think they'd ever come across anything like it before, the sight of a large group of women who were well organized, well able to look after themselves, and well able to express their opinions of us and to us with some strength of feeling. A lot of the men had never seen women behaving like that, and couldn't get out of their minds the idea there must be some men somewhere in the background who were directing and controlling them. If it hadn't been so unpleasant and serious it might almost have been funny. It was unpleasant because here we were, facing women who were mostly our own age, and we didn't know what they were going to do. It made us nervous and edgy. On one occasion they all came up very close to the fence and started shaking it: it really did look as though it was going to come down. What exactly we'd have done if there had been a mass break-in I'm not at all certain. Obviously there are contingency plans, our commanding officer knows exactly what he'll do in every possible circumstance. But they weren't revealed to us beforehand, so we were in the position of not knowing what the next order would be. We just hoped it wouldn't be anything dreadful.

I know it was said in Parliament that if necessary the soldiers would be ordered to fire. I can't be specific about this, but I don't feel they would pour a volley of shots into a group of unarmed demonstrators, I really don't. I have to say however that I could be wrong: the ultimate orders may have been of that kind, but personally I doubt it.

I think it's very unfortunate that the situation ever arose, that soldiers should have had to go there to help hold the security of the perimeter. I won't say it's the fault of the women, and if they hadn't brought it about it wouldn't have happened. I've heard that argument advanced, but I think it's a weak one, on a par with the things the police say like "If you've done nothing wrong, you've nothing to be afraid of if you're arrested." It had happened that someone in the police had felt they might not be able to contain any larger number of demonstrators if they suddenly appeared, so they asked the Army for help. I suspect the soldiers were there as a deterrent, and I don't think there was ever any intention of them attempting to disperse the women outside the fence. As far as I'm aware there was no physical contact between soldiers and demonstrators: all the arrests were made by the police.

All the same, it was a very serious situation. In Ireland on the streets, because of the numbers both of civilians and soldiers, it would have been in the same category as a major riot. I think credit has to be given to the women for the fact that they kept the demonstration peaceful. I suppose to an Army officer it would be thinking the unthinkable to allow oneself to believe they might in fact have a point in what they were doing and saying, that our country would be if not safer, then in no way less safe if the Americans took their missiles away. I've heard it argued in the mess that these things are here in this country at the invitation and with the agreement of the British government. But from what little I've read about the subject, I think it was never debated in Parliament. So I don't think it could be claimed it's the will of the majority of the people. Having said that though, it has to be said it might be. The only way we'll find that out is if there's a referendum, which won't happen, or if a different party is elected to govern and has made it one of its election pledges that it'll do something to alter the situation.

I think a lot of the soldiers felt not only disturbed by the sight of the demonstrating women, but rather uneasy at the whole situation. Having had experience in other countries of trouble with the civilian population, some of them thought they could well be in for something in the nature of a fight. Apart from a few lunatics who'd slaughter their own grandmothers if they were told to, most of them had their moments of thinking, and wondered what might happen and what kind of position they might find themselves in. Personally I noticed that a number of soldiers who were usually the jolliest and noisiest were, at Greenham, very quiet and seemed to have been preoccupied with their own thoughts.

iii.   All those selfish bitches: Susan Shaw, private's wife

— They do honestly, they really drive me spitting mad all those selfish bitches at Greenham Common. Our husbands had to go down there and sort them out, and if I could've got my hands on them I would've killed them, really I would. Some of us were even thinking of hiring a coach privately among ourselves and going down there for the day and telling them what we thought about them. We got as far as booking the coach, but then one of the sergeants' wives came round us all and said it'd be better if we didn't get ourselves involved, it'd look bad in the newspapers if soldiers' wives went there and had their own demonstration. So after a bit of arguing between ourselves we decided not to. That's one of the things of being an Army wife, you're not free to do what you want like everyone else: it's always got to be taken into account what effect it's going to have on the Army.

I suppose the main trouble was the men had only come back two days before from an exercise in Wales. They'd been away over a week, and we was looking forward to having them here for a week or two, they've been away such a lot this year already. They come back on the Tuesday or was it the Wednesday, and we'd all got plans made for the weekend: going to see parents, taking the kids to see grandparents, going out on the Saturday night, all the sorts of things we hadn't done for ages. And then there you are, less than forty-eight hours later they're on standby, then within twelve hours of that away they go to Greenham. Everyone was bloody furious about it.

To my way of thinking the main point about it is that if it hadn't been for those women I'd have had Barry at home for a few days, but because of them he had to go away again. They have the right to their own ideas, after all that's what this country's all about isn't it? But if ordinary people don't agree with something, they get up a march and have a meeting in Trafalgar Square or somewhere like that. They don't go out and have a demonstration in the middle of the countryside, and make everyone else have to go and deal with them. They don't think what amount of inconvenience they're putting everyone else to, no that never crosses their minds: all they think about is getting themselves in the newspapers and on the television. I saw one who was interviewed when my husband was there: she stood there and she said "I have to do what I have to do." I nearly threw that clock through the television set. I thought "You shitty cow, my husband has to do what he has to do too, only nobody interviews him about it for the television, oh no!"

I'm not sure what it is they're protesting about anyway. We've got our own nuclear weapons and it stands to reason if other countries have got them we've got to have them too. Or are they saying we shouldn't have them, the Russians should be just let come in and walk all over us? If that's what they really think they must be even dafter than I thought.

When my Barry came back he said he'd been talking to some of the policemen there, and he'd found out they'd all volunteered for duty at Greenham because the rates of pay they get there are so terrific. They get special allowances for being away from home, for working unsocial hours, for working Saturdays and Sundays: you can't imagine how many different items they get extra money for, and it all tots up to a whacking sum, £80 a day I heard. Our boys don't get a penny extra, they get the same pay for a day's work as they always do. I think that's very unfair, specially the "unsocial hours" bit. You wouldn't think it was so bad when your husband was away if you thought there was going to be a bit extra in the housekeeping for the rest of the week, but for soldiers there's no question of that sort of thing.

I've never read anything about the women much. The first time some of them were on television I was quite surprised, some of them sounded they were people who'd had quite good educations. A lot were punks with their heads shaved and that sort of thing, but there was some quite elderly women who spoke as though they came from good class backgrounds. Those are the ones I find hardest of all to understand. OK, if you're a kid and you want to wear fancy clothes and have the latest hair styles, I can understand that, I was a bit that way myself when I was their age. You think it's funny, you think you're doing something a bit daring if you're attracting attention to yourself. But if you've had all that money spent on your education, then I think it's disgusting you can't find anything better to do than make an exhibition of yourself for the television people. Some of them were shouting and pushing and screaming, laying down in the mud and all things like that. That's not the way to behave if you've had a good education is it? I thought the point of an education was that it taught you how to argue with people and get them to see your point of view, not make you into someone going around causing trouble all the time.

I think if a lot of people had realized how much trouble those women were causing ordinary decent soldiers, making them have to go and stand on guard duties out in the cold and all the rest of it, well if people realized that they'd pass a law saying those women should go home. I think a lot of them would go home, if they knew what they were doing to ordinary people like our husbands and us. My Mandy said to me "Where's Daddy gone now?" She's only seven, and she was very disappointed because I'd told her we were going to go to the seaside with her Daddy at the weekend. I didn't know what to say. We've always told her her Daddy's in the Army and sometimes he has to go away to fight people, or to help defend people against those who're trying to attack them. But for that Greenham business, honestly what can you say?

iv. Utterable contempt: Jennifer Long, captain's wife

– For me it was the most difficult time I've ever had since Alan and I were married. I've always accepted that his job was his job, that wherever he went as a soldier he was being a professional. I hope the modern Army no longer functions on a basis of "Their's not to wonder why, Their's but to do or die", though there've been odd occasions when I've been a bit doubtful about the sort of thing he's been asked to do. But it's never troubled my conscience greatly: I always felt on balance that because he was a soldier, it justified what he had to do. But when he came and said they were going to Greenham, there was really an awful silence descended on us. We know each other well enough for there to be certain things we don't need to say: and we both knew this was one of those times, only quite the biggest and most important we've ever had. We'd talked of course, who hasn't, about the Greenham women: and Alan isn't entirely sympathetic to their point of view, to what they're trying to achieve and how they're going about it. I'm much more in their direction myself and I've never made any secret of it to him.

I feel nuclear weapons are so awful and so indiscriminate that there couldn't ever be any justification for their use. It's not like the old wars when you had soldiers fighting each other on the battlefields, and there were rules observed by both sides as to what was legitimate to do and what wasn't. This is something absolutely different: there won't be two lots of soldiers facing each other, it'll be entirely indiscriminate. The casualties will include, and everybody knows it, they'll include civilians of all kinds: old people, children, babies, the sick and ill: everybody and everything will be involved, and there can't be and won't be any picking and choosing of intended victims. They say nuclear weapons are only intended as a deterrent and nobody will ever really use them. If you think that, then the enemy's deterrent to you, or your deterrent to the enemy, has lost its point. The mere fact you have these weapons and would even contemplate using them is only a credible deterrent if it's certain you'll use them. And we hear from the so-called statesmen involved that what is certain is that what they call "mutually assured destruction" will happen. That seems to me to be absolutely immoral, and I don't think anybody should have any part of it.

Alan and I have never gone along with the belief there were things that shouldn't be talked about: whether they're to do with our families, our feelings about each other, or our own ideas on every subject under the sun. We try to respect one another's points of view, and we don't have rows. But as far as Greenham's concerned, my attitude has always been I'm on the side of the women. I may not always agree with some of their more extravagant actions, but I entirely respect their sincerity and I often wish more women would join them. I think men have made a complete cock-up of the world, and the way they're going at the moment they look as though they're going to kill themselves and everyone else. So unless somebody comes up with a better solution, I think the women who're demonstrating at Greenham are at least forcing people to think: and that's a good thing whichever way you look at it. To be perfectly honest about it I've been tempted more than once to go down to Greenham myself and spend at least one night there, just as a mark of solidarity with them. It's not much, God knows it's not really anything at all except perhaps something for the benefit of my own conscience. And it's hovering in the back of my mind, and I know it's in the back of Alan's mind too, that I might actually do it.

I'd have to go without telling a soul where I was going, or who I was. I have to remember I'm the wife of a soldier in a position of authority, and that it's simply not possible for me to do something of that sort, however much I want to for the sake of my own beliefs, and him to keep his career. This is the kind of thing which makes being a soldier's wife very very difficult indeed. But I don't admire myself for dithering. I think such behaviour can only be described as one I look upon with utterable contempt.

v. And furthermore

– I don't agree with nuclear weapons at all. If there was a Green party in this country I would vote for them. I see they have got into our Parliament in Germany, they are like a peace party and they oppose all types of war. Obviously with my husband a soldier I can't oppose war and I don't, I think sometimes it's justified. But using nuclear weapons and wiping out whole populations, I think this is wrong. My husband was one of those who had to go to Greenham to guard the perimeter fence, and I said to him "If you ever so much as spit at one of those women, don't tell me about it because I'll have no more to do with you."

(Lisa J., private's wife)

There's no logic to nuclear warfare. The received philosophy is we're entitled to use such weapons *in extremis*, and we accept our enemies the Russians may do the same. But I wasn't trained as a professional soldier to indulge in, or do anything which might bring about, the wholesale slaughter of civilians, the wholesale destruction of entire cities and indeed of entire countries. There are rules to warfare, and they should be obeyed. I think CND have a point when they say nuclear warfare would be a crime against humanity. I'm not by any means the only person I know in this regiment who is sympathetic to CND.

In the mess, although I make no secret of my sympathy, it's not a subject very frequently talked about: and several of my colleagues seem to think it's tantamount to being a member of the Communist party.

(Richard P., lieutenant)

– I've nothing against these women and I don't think they're all communists or any of that nonsense. I just think they're completely misguided. They haven't got a proper idea of why we're defending the cruise missiles, and they don't see that if we hadn't got them we'd be entirely defenceless if anyone wanted to attack us. We have to keep them as a deterrent to our enemies.

(*John R., lance corporal*)

— Before we went to Greenham, the platoon commanders gave talks to their troops explaining why we were going. It had to be made clear to them what they were being asked to do, what orders might possibly be given, and why. In the modern Army you can't any longer rely on men blindly obeying: especially if it's something like possibly shooting at civilians, it really has to be got over to them so they understand why they're there and what if necessary they might be called on to do. The way ours approached it was to encourage questions and discussion after he'd talked. There were quite a few of the soldiers who couldn't see it could ever be right under any circumstances to shoot unarmed people. I'm not permitted to specify the exact circumstances under which such a thing could happen: but I can tell you, so long as it's not attributed to me personally, that I think there's no doubt a situation could have arisen in which shots could have been fired.

(*Arthur J., sergeant*)

— I had the impression when they were giving us talks and asking us to ask questions they were sorting us out. I mean listening to what we said very carefully, identifying the ones who'd shoot anyone without argument when an order was given, and those who had doubts about it. I think if the operational situation had arisen, those of us who'd asked questions would be kept at the back if you get my meaning.

(*Michael R., corporal*)

— I came back from Greenham really disillusioned with the Army. I thought it was disgusting we should be mucked about like that, sent there at hardly any notice because the fucking police couldn't do their job properly and so we had to go and help them out. And they was all on terrific extra money, and what did we get for it? Fuck all.

(*Jack B., private*)

— I think most of us were very angry about being sent to Greenham because it was such a disruption of our routine. No one seriously thought for one moment we'd have any kind of confrontation with the women. Our job was just to stand there and if they'd any such idea in their mind dissuade them from trying to get into the base in large numbers. That's not what soldiering is, and it's not what we'd been trained for. Our role is either to fight, or assist the civil power in the maintaining of order, or in extreme cases such as strikes for example, keep certain essential services functioning. There was absolutely nothing of that sort at Greenham, it was a complete and utter waste of time. I also question the morality of it: I think it was entirely wrong to send the Army there. It was an American base, therefore it was the job of the Americans to defend it. Let them be the ones who attracted the insults: that would be more realistic, and to involve the British Army was fudging the issue. If people don't want American missiles here, one of the things that would get them support would be if the Americans were seen to be defending them themselves.

(*Peter N., lieutenant*)

– It was all a laugh was Greenham. Not a fucking thing happened, we just stood around like charlies. I don't reckon those women are such stupid people at all, I can see their point of view. I'm a bit thick on that kind of subject and I'd never given any thought to it before. When I went there and saw the conditions they were living in, I thought it showed they must be serious people. I don't know whether I agree with them or not, but I do have respect for them.

(*Stanley T., private*)

– I think at Greenham we was just being used as cheap labour. We was sent there and told we had to keep the perimeter intact, that our job was to put people off trying to get in. I didn't agree with it at all because you never know it might have come to a scrap. I don't fancy the idea of fighting with a load of women all screaming and yelling. One of the units next to our section had fires they could stand round, and boxes they could take shelter in, but we had nothing. Our sergeant said it showed they weren't as professional as us. I thought, "Yes mate, what you mean is they haven't professional flannellers like you, you big cunt."

(*Eddie M., lance corporal*)

– Troops at Greenham firing on civilians? I don't think the idea was meant seriously for a moment, from all I've read and heard I can't envisage any such situation ever arising. I don't think most soldiers would obey an order to fire on unarmed women, and anyway I don't think they would ever be given such an order. It would lead to such an appalling and unimaginable situation in the country it's quite beyond thinking of.

(Michael S., second lieutenant)

— In the Army you have the whole strata of society, and that means you're bound to have a proportion, even if only a very small one, of radical dissenters. After all this is a great English tradition.

This means at times like Greenham, we come face to face with a disobedient civil population. I've never wanted to think of myself as 100 per cent on the side of the Establishment, and I don't think I would have been what's called "reliable" if there'd been any serious trouble there. I do hope though the women wouldn't take that as any sign of encouragement, because I know a good number of officers who'd be entirely "reliable". I would hate to think what could happen when they were in charge.

(David D., captain)

— I would certainly carry out any order so long as it was legal: and I would take it it was legal if my superiors gave the order that peace protestors were to be shot at. The fact that I personally happen to disagree with them makes it slightly easier I suppose. I'd have given such an order at Greenham if I'd been called on to do so. I'm part of the government's arm of government, and if such a horrible situation ever arose that we were in conflict with the civilian population, I'd do what the government said.

(Mark W., lieutenant)

— It all went off very quietly, and in my experience it was the first time we'd ever been deployed in England against people. It caused a good deal of heart-searching and thinking at all levels: the implications of it were very serious. You accepted it in Northern Ireland, across the water and in a different country: but when you come face to face with civil disobedience here in your own country, things look different. In Ireland though the protestors and demonstrators were violent, they used great violence against us, so it wasn't difficult to justify violence against them. But these women were something different.

(Jim D., sergeant)

– We had very little idea what was going to happen there, it was all very peaceful. All the women were pleasant and friendly towards us, at times it was just like a big picnic. There we were, soldiers inside the base and protestors outside: so so long as it stayed like that things were fine. But what was expected of us if they came in through the fence? Were we going to physically fight our own population? We chewed the fat over that a lot when we were there.

(*Mike B., corporal*)

– You had to explain to the soldiers it had nothing whatever to do with the rights or wrongs of nuclear weapons. It was our job to protect that base because it was a military installation. We tried to put it over to the troops by saying they should look on it as an aerodrome or an ordnance depot or whatever they liked, where people had to be stopped before they got in. A few of the soldiers did express misgivings, they said "Sir, we don't agree with this at all." That really made you think: you'd explained it all to them and they still didn't accept it. Could have meant trouble, but fortunately it never came to it.

(*Roger S., lieutenant*)

– Only about a week or so before we went there was a downright disgusting article in one of the daily papers about the women, attacking them and saying they were whores, lesbians, all divorced or separated and unhappy women who were neglecting their husbands and children, and everything else. It was a really bitter attack, and I was surprised how badly it went down in the mess. Some of the young subalterns who hadn't the brains to know better were sniggering about it, but Bill said out loud and clear when he read it "You know, I admire these women. I admire them for their conviction and their integrity. If that's what they believe and feel is the only appropriate action to take, then good luck to them. It takes a lot of guts." About six or seven others all immediately said "Hear hear, yes, good luck to them. They're making people think, you've got to admire them for that." So that gives you an idea.

(*Alan B., major*)

– All those absolutely ghastly women, if only you could have seen them! They looked the absolute dregs. I wasn't in the least surprised to read a newspaper article about them where it said most of them were not only lesbians, but vegetarian lesbians. So that gives you some idea doesn't it?

(*Jeremy L., second lieutenant*)

14 In Command: The General

— I am a soldier, above all, because I believe deeply in people and in the natural freedom which should be given to them. They shouldn't in their actions one upon another rub up against other people in society, so we have to have some form of sensible level of rules of behaviour. I think this is understood in a democracy: but in the communist world it's gone far too far and become a denial of freedom. I think we've got the balance, imperfect though it may be, much better in what's known as "the free world".

My own life as a soldier gives me enormous pleasure. It brings me into contact with — indeed it's all about — people at all levels, and it gives me great satisfaction to provide for others the same satisfaction of achievement. We've only one life to live, and we need such challenges, intellectual or physical or a balance of the two. In the Army we have the sense of the importance of achieving things in life, not just sitting looking at a television set or complaining about others. I like to have a positive approach myself, and I like to see it in others. And where I do see it in others, I'll forgive them virtually anything in terms of things going wrong, because they are trying in a good and positive way. In the widest sense, you know, democracy is a fallible thing — but it's also a very marvellous thing: democracy is people trying together to achieve a better life in as free a society as possible. I like that, I like protecting that: it's probably the greatest challenge of all. And I don't hate the Russians: I suspect in fact I'd like them a lot as individuals. The British soldier has always had a certain affection and respect for worthy enemies. But it happens that the corporate Russian attitude, the attitude to life within the communist world, takes away the kind of freedoms that are so precious to us in western society.

I believe that within the context of the present day world the Army's both moral and necessary. We start from the premise that we're a democracy and as such will never be an aggressor. Our moral case rests to my mind utterly on this fact, that we're not an attacking organization, we are a defending organization. If our lives and our society are threatened, then we have to prepare to be aggressive in order to achieve the defence of freedom and our way of life. I believe our society fights very well in defence of its freedoms, but it takes time sometimes to understand what is at stake, and that needs to be understood if it's to fight well. Once it is understood, then our society is a very redoubtable adversary. In other words it prefers to have the moral and emotional impetus of being in the right. I believe as a fighting man that in an idealistic sense our Army is a deterrent against others taking action against us to take from us the way of life we prefer. It's on that basis only that I believe there really is justification for defence. If we were in a world where everyone was prepared to respect others and not try to take their freedoms away, then we wouldn't need armed forces: but I'm afraid my judgment is that human nature's got a very long way to go indeed before it reaches that point.

I think from a purely military point of view a volunteer Army such as we have today is an excellent thing. It allows one to create professional standards that are higher than in a conscript army: and it allows one to do more with less, in terms of performance, because the men have wider capabilities. They can handle two or three jobs rather than one: indeed they need to have that sort of challenge, of widening training and wider scope for what they can do. In another sense also it's important in that where the national interest is at stake the issues may be highly emotional: and a regular Army, and the other forces, can be launched more readily and easily because it consists of volunteers who are ready for action, rather than a national service that's less well trained.

So that's the principal reason that I think a volunteer service has a real virtue. But in another sense I've always felt too that there are dangers. The armed services need to have a strong link with society: they need to be known to society, and they need to have the respect of society, because if they don't, then we don't recruit effectively or get the right sort of people. And equally society needs to understand us. In order for that to happen a constant flow of those who've been in the services is needed to go out into society and talk about the

Army. Two-way communication is very important. With a national service or conscript army you'd get the flow of information which keeps the services in the public eye in a personal way, which is more difficult with a limited size of Army such as we have now.

Another point I'd like to make is that society needs to be involved in its own defence. There's been a long national tradition of the British having services, volunteer and limited in size, that have lived abroad for much of their lives. Services that in a sense can be left to get on with defence until there comes a war: and then they're expected to bear the brunt, in the initial phases at least. That's not the way society on the continent has mostly been organized: it's usually had some form of conscription where there's involvement by the whole of society. I'm thinking of countries such as Germany, France, or Switzerland, where society understands defence and contributes towards it with their sons and daughters. We don't have this in our country, and I think therefore we have to be careful to keep our links open, give advertisement of what our services do, and remind the country constantly that we are *their* Army. We are the British Army, belonging to the British people, born from them and serving them in every sense: and we have to be careful this is never forgotten. So I think I wouldn't be averse to some form of limited National Service, I do see certain virtues in it.

It would have some advantages to the Army too: it would open the eyes of the Army to society. Some people in some places almost certainly don't have their eyes sufficiently open. I feel that's because we're such a strongly hierarchical organization, so complete in ourselves. We're an island unto ourselves in many ways. We have very strong family habits and disciplines, and so unless we're careful we do tend to look inward. The Army takes great trouble to try and defeat this, by making officers and NCOs read newspapers and study the news, go out into society, go and recruit. But it's endemic in any volunteer army that it's liable to be a bit inward-looking, and pursue excellence and at times even slightly look down on others. Anyone who suggested we're slightly inward-looking and inbred could probably prove the point to a degree. It's not widespread – but we do have to watch it, there's no doubt about that.

There are stereotypes, and I think many soldiers *want* to be stereotypes in the sense that they want to conform: we're a very disciplined organization so one expects conformists in it. You start with the fact we salute each other, that we have a hierarchical organization and we respect that organization. This is one of the prices one pays for high standards of discipline and performance in battle: that these have to be trained for in peace. But I believe what we have to do is to leaven that with a constant awareness that we are stereotyped to a degree. For instance one of the clear signs of a soldier at a cocktail party is he'll start to talk about his job using abbreviations which no one else understands. I myself am against using abbreviations in that way, because it separates us from the rest of society if people don't understand what we're talking about. We should be conscious that society likes to hear and to understand, and if it doesn't understand it gets bored. That sort of awareness is what we try to educate our officers in: we actually push them out into society, in terms of giving them university educations, sending them out to visit schools and so forth, so that they're conscious of it. I'm afraid you pay a price for being the Army, the same price you would pay in being a member of a church. If that's being stereotype, then I think we have to bear it to a degree: but we have to make sure it isn't destructive of the human strength of the organization.

We have to have our minds open about other people and about our own organization. It can stop one thinking clearly if all one accepts is that the traditions and systems of the past were entirely excellent. Perhaps they were in their day – but perhaps circumstances have changed now, and we should adjust to that. I say "adjust" rather than destroy and break them up. And in order to do so one has to have officers and men who think for themselves within the broad corporate discipline of the Army. I think one of the characteristics of the soldier of the 1980s is he's much more prepared to think for himself, and he's much more encouraged to do so than say twenty, thirty or forty years ago when I first joined the Army. I find that very encouraging.

When we first met I told you what I was doing and how in some ways I hoped to do it. You replied that you thought it was a good idea: why did you think it was?

– As I said, I hope it will allow soldiers to express a little bit about themselves to an independent observer.

From the top of the Army all the way down, there's a momentum to our attitude and a positiveness to it, I believe the country could well observe with benefit. It's implicit in the way we're organized and trained, but it's also actually in our hearts and in our minds, this corporate desire and this individual desire to make the whole thing succeed. We're not perfect, we're imperfect as individuals: but every so often we rise above ourselves as an organisation, particularly when we're challenged. I believe the Army likes challenge, in fact revels in it, because it knows it's positive and forward-looking.

And we have a pretty complete society within each part of the Army: in other words, we foster and care and take interest in our fan.ilies and in soldiers throughout their Army life and after they leave the Army, so that when they come back they undoubtedly feel great nostalgia. I'd like to see more of that in civilian companies throughout the country in the great companies that lead in industry. I'd like to see more evidence that the managers and directors occasionally go down and walk with affection and liking among the men they lead. So I believe soldiers talking to you can communicate the spirit we have, that we have a moral and social message for the country.

15 Soldier, Soldier

— I like the life. These barracks he's at, we're near a nice town: I like going on the bus and looking round the shops, and there's a good swimming baths there. He's away just now in Cyprus, and I think it's much worse for him than it is for me. At least I've got all our own things around me. There's a terrific lot laid on for the wives: on Monday afternoons there's keep fit, Wednesdays and Fridays I go to squash, Tuesday afternoon we have the wives' social club. On the first Tuesday every month there we have an activity, say a film night plus a Chinese meal. I've a little girl of three, and she goes to the play school run in the social club hall by the Army.

It might sound awful, but I quite enjoy Terry going away. Two weeks here, two weeks there: what is it, absence makes the heart or something, I do, I agree with that.

(Barbara L., lance corporal's wife)

— Boredom I'd say is the worst problem when my husband's away. The children are in boarding school so I don't even have them. I really never know what to do with myself, and I can't get a job because when he comes home I like to be with him. It's the going away, coming back, going away: a few days, a few weeks, you can't ever work out anything satisfactory. You can't say to an employer "I'll work for you for six months, or three months, or six weeks, or six days, when my husband's away." No employer's going to look at that. I don't feel I could even involve myself in voluntary work or something of that sort, because you've got to be reliable about the times when you'll be available haven't you?

(Shirley R., sergeant's wife)

– I've a terrific lot of friends with the other wives. We do lots of things together, have cups of coffee, go to the social club where we natter and chatter and gossip. I do, I really enjoy the life.

My parents didn't like it when it came to me going to Ireland, but I said to them "I've no choice, I've got to go, I'm in the Army." That's the way I look at it. They say you don't just marry your husband you marry the Army don't they? And I'm happy for it to be like that.

(Jean C., corporal's wife)

– To be perfectly honest I would prefer it if he had another job. When he's away I miss him, I feel incomplete as a person, and I don't feel I've much of a life with only the children here. As far as I'm concerned life comes to a standstill then. It's important to me to know he's happy doing what he is doing, but when helpful people say "Oh haven't you got used to him going away yet, surely in time you get used to it?" I get very irritated with them. I don't see I shall or should. If you get to the point where you don't really care if your husband's away, it seems to me that's not a good thing.

(Margaret P., captain's wife)

– I don't think it's true you're married to the Army. You have your own life, his going away is part of it and you're not part of it. In England he goes to work, he comes home at the end of the day, and that's that. Sometimes he has to work at weekends but so do other people in other jobs. I can't say I don't like it, I can't say that even I mind it, because I don't. If I had done, Bill would have left the Army. The separations always seem to bring us closer together. We've been married for thirteen years, and we look forward to each other's company. That's the only way to deal with it I think when he has to go away: not look on the black side and think it's awful, but look forward to him coming back again. We've our two children and our house and everything. He and I've not had an argument between us in over the year he's been home, so there must be something to be said for the life mustn't there? And I've a little job of my own part-time at the supermarket so I have pocket money, and it lets me feel just that bit independent, you know?

(Betty D., sergeant's wife)

– My husband's life revolves around the Army. He's just a private and I'm just a private's wife, but we have a house and he has a steady job, and how many can say that these days? I quite like the regular separations, perhaps we're a bit unusual like that. When he comes

back it's like a second honeymoon. I've a friend whose husband's in
a different battalion, and she and I have this agreement we take each
other's kids for the first day or two after a return, so we can be on
our own with our husbands. But I definitely don't like six months'
separation, that's hard. The funny thing is after that happened last
year, when he came home we were both so shy we didn't even have
sex on the first night.

(Jackie M., private's wife)

– For me the hardest thing is being so far away from my own family:
I've two brothers and two sisters, and we were all always very close.
When my husband goes away, even if it's only for a few days, I'm on
the phone nearly every evening a long time to one or other of them.
My husband gets cross when he hears about it, because of the
expense. But I don't know many of the other wives here: they
probably think I'm stand-offish, but it's only that I'm shy. And I
don't expect they want to hear all my woes and moans about my
husband being away, they're in the same position, so I put it all on
my family. I expect I'll get used to it, but I haven't anything like got
used to it so far.

(Pat D., private's wife)

– When the Army says he's got to go he's got to go, so no wife can
ever have a settled existence. She's got a lot of adjustments to make
– to him going away, to him coming back, to living on her own
while he's away, to uprooting her home and moving wherever it is
the Army's said he's got to go next. You need to be a certain type of
woman to cope with all those things. I don't know what the word is,
it might be "placid", it might be "cow-like": you'd have to think
hard to find an exact word. Your children suffer from not having a
life of their own, they're as much part of Army existence as you are.
To give just a tiny example, they can't stick drawing pins in the walls
of their rooms if they want to put posters up. So on one hand you've
got advantages, on the other you've got quite a lot of disadvantages
that other people don't have. You work it all out on balance, and
you decide you'll settle for this. I think that's true of most women in
most marriages: they settle for it and all it entails, because they
prefer it to being on their own.

(Freda S., sergeant's wife)

– He's got three more years to do, and then he has to decide whether
to sign on for some more. I hope he does, because I don't want him

to come out because I'm scared of the insecurity. I come from a little village in Norfolk, I go home when he's away, and when I see my friends of my own age who are married I think their lives are boring. I've been in Germany, I've been in Northern Ireland, and now here, so I've had quite a bit of variety already. I think it's nice to live in different places: how many women could say they'd lived in three different countries in five years?

(Mary G., corporal's wife)

– I get a bit tired of it when I hear some of the women complaining what a hard time they have financially, how they can't go out for meals except once in a blue moon and that sort of thing. They're often the same ones you see going around in new clothes, or they've bought a second-hand motor-car or a video, or they're going somewhere special with the kids when the husband comes home, and you find they've spent hundreds of pounds on it. Anyone can live a decent life on Army pay if they're sensible about money. It might not be the lap of luxury, but you can get by. If you really can't, there's plenty of places in town who want part-time women cleaners for a couple of hours at night or something of that sort, so you can make up a bit of extra.

(Jill L., private's wife)

– I remember Steve once said at breakfast table he was NFA, you know "No Fixed Abode". I was quite hurt about it, because I'd always tried to make a home for him wherever we were. I shouldn't have been hurt: he'd just come back from the latest of a whole series of exercises which had all kept him away ages, he was only expressing how he was feeling. But it did make me realize that since he lived that sort of life, nothing I could do would make a lot of difference. He's an Army man, and that's what the Army does for you, gives you that kind of feeling about yourself.

(Nancy E., captain's wife)

– Fidelity's a problem on both sides. After all when your husband's away you have the time and the opportunity: and when he's away so does he, especially in a foreign country. He meets a woman, they take a fancy to each other, they have an affair: who's going to know about it? When he comes to the end of his time there, he's never going to see her again. I don't think it's surprising it happens, sometimes I think it's surprising it doesn't happen more. When you're lonely, a little love affair can be very enjoyable.

(*Anne R., sergeant major's wife*)

— I think some of the good-looking girls have a bit of a hard time fending off the men, the civilian men who know their husbands are away. Men have all got this idea haven't they of a woman "She must be missing it" and all that sort of stuff? They've got wives of their own mind you, but they're offering to do us the favour of going to bed with us so we won't be lonely. The Army says it encourages soldiers to get married and it does: but I sometimes think that's the wrong policy, it ought in the main to be a single man's Army. I mean when you think about it, what sort of a life, particularly a sex life, do you have when all the dates for it are decided in advance for you?

(*Audrey W., sergeant major's wife*)

— You get really annoyed, at least I do: I'll be say in the corporals' mess and some girl who's in the Army herself comes up to you and she says "Your husband's fine." It's someone you've never set eyes on in your life, and she tells you she met him a couple of weeks ago in Cyprus or wherever, he asked her to look you up and give you his love. This has happened to me two times: the first time I blew Gary up about it, so of course he said "Well if you don't want to hear from me I won't send any messages. But you wouldn't like it if I'd met somebody and you'd heard about it from somebody else, and I'd not said anything about it would you?"

(*Janet R., corporal's wife*)

— I hated thinking what he might be doing when he was away. There's nobody knows him better than me, well there isn't when you've lived with somebody for a long time as their wife is there? He's always had this thing that he can't go to sleep at night until he's had it, you know what I mean? So you think when he's away "What's he doing about it tonight?" It's not a nice thing to say, but you do think about it especially when that's what he's always told you. The first year or two we were married, we had some rows because I asked him, or I made hints that I'd like to ask him. Since then I've never mentioned it because it's not worth the rows. You can't help having the thoughts though.

(*Pauline P., private's wife*)

— Once where we lived it was very difficult. There was a gas leak, I could smell gas, and the man from the Gas Board didn't come till quite late. He worked very hard and he was tired, so I offered him a cup of coffee. We were sitting drinking it in the sitting room when one of my next-door neighbours walked in through the back door. There was nothing going on, but she didn't help by looking all embarrassed and saying what she'd come about wasn't important, she'd come back the following day. The grapevine started working overtime, within a couple of days it was all over the estate I'd had the gas man in at eleven o'clock at night.

(Mary N., lance corporal's wife)

– He's in Belize and I know there are brothels there and things. And he went to Mexico for his leave. I don't blame him for going but it's only natural you wonder what he might be up to, specially when he's writing telling you about the beaches and the holiday resorts and that sort of thing. You wonder if he's meeting beautiful girls, or even not-so-beautiful girls. And he's on holiday and what he does is something you're never going to hear about. You can, you can work yourself up into quite a state about it if you want to do.

(Rita D., Private's wife)

– The bloody Families Officers seem to think they're responsible for our morals while our husbands are away. They come round for a "friendly" chat with you, and you get the feeling they're prying into your private life: whether you're going out at night, whether some man's coming round a bit often. They say things like "You've been having trouble with your telly have you, I hear the van was round three times last week." They make heavy hints about how tough it is for the soldiers when they're away, and how they might hear their wives might be getting a bit involved with someone. It's a laugh the way they're so bloody unsubtle about it: they say "I know you wouldn't be involved in anything of that sort Mrs So-and-So, but people do gossip don't they?"

(Jenny L., corporal's wife)

– You handle the kids the best you can yourself. I don't agree with asking your husband to straighten them out if they've been giving you trouble while he's been away. "Why've you been giving your Mum a hard time?" When he's been away a good while and they've been looking forward to him coming back, you can't have him starting off at them like that can you? They'd soon start resenting him coming home. If he's been away any length of time he's a kind of interloper in the home anyway, who disturbs the routine. I notice that our eldest girl who's eleven, she can't help it but she resents the attention I give Derek when he's back, because all my attention's been focused on her. She's been my friend, she's been the person I treat like a grown-up and talk to about problems with her brother and sister, or how to make the money go round and that sort of thing. So it's hard for her when Derek's back, and suddenly she and I are not on those terms any more. It's Derek I discuss things with, and if I didn't he'd resent it himself. So it's tricky.

(*Lorna W., captain's wife*)

– They say you never learn don't they, well that's true in my case. I married a soldier when I was eighteen. I was pregnant but that didn't make any difference, I never asked him to marry me: we got married because we loved each other. We had two more kids and they've all grown up into really lovely kids, I'm not just saying that because they're mine. But after nine years we broke up. You can't say it was entirely his fault, you can't say it was entirely my fault. There's a lot of strain put on a marriage, your husband going away, you having to accept the Army comes first in his life and all the rest of it. I think there was one or two others he'd had a little thing with but then you expect that with men.

And there was a bloke I got involved with while my husband was away. I tried to give him up when Alan came back, but I was so bloody miserable it was obvious to Alan there'd been someone else. We sat down and talked about it, and we agreed from every point of view it was better to bring the marriage to an end. It meant I had to move out of the quarter, but I had my Mum's to go to and Alan went back in barracks. It wasn't quite as friendly as I'm telling you makes it sound but on the whole it wasn't too bad: divorce is never a very nice business is it?

I blamed the Army for what had happened, and I told my mother and everyone that it was impossible to have a stable happy marriage with a soldier. Then two years later what did I do? I went and married another soldier. Like I say, you never learn. He was very good about the children, I can't complain about the way he's treated them. Perhaps it's that he's four years younger than me, I don't know. But now I'm in exactly the same position again. It isn't working out, he and I have separated, and I'm back at my Mum's again. It's true you see, you can't make a marriage with a soldier: or well I can't, and you'd think I'd have learned it first time. Exactly the same thing: him having a bit on the side when he goes away, me getting mixed up with someone else. This new bloke's not a soldier, so at least you could say perhaps I was learning: the only trouble is though he's already married as well. I don't know, what a tangle.

(Tina B., corporal's wife)

– You get used to doing things on your own and you get into a routine. The other day the vacuum cleaner broke down, so I got a screwdriver and dismantled it to see what was wrong. He said he'd put it right for me: I wasn't trying to be difficult, I said it was all right I could do it myself. Which I could, I'd done it before when he was away. He went straight up the wall, he said I made him look a fool in front of the children. So we had a big big row about who was going to repair the vacuum cleaner for God's sake.

(Jean A., private's wife)

– It can really get nasty. He knows if you do anything he objects to – I don't mean playing around, I mean perhaps just going out with a friend – he can always threaten you that he'll leave you and go back into barracks. There's no answer to his question "And where'll that leave you?" You know where, out on the street.

(Lisa M., private's wife)

– The first time he went away after Ian was born, the night he came back he got up to him because he was crying. Ian was frightened because he didn't know who he was. That was a bad moment and Peter took it rather hard. He also didn't like it that I'd changed all the cupboards round and he couldn't find anything. It took us at least two weeks before he felt he belonged in the house: he'd been away six months, which is a long time. Funny things too: I'd be doing the washing up and I'd turn round and bang into him because he was standing behind me doing the drying up. Or once I went upstairs to the loo and its door was locked: I knew the children were out, and I couldn't think what'd happened. I banged on the door and I said "Whos' in there, who is it?" That was the first time we'd had a long separation and one didn't notice the effect it'd had.

(Sally J., major's wife)

– You're not an individual, you're a wife of: you accept it's got to be like that in the Army, but there's nothing that says you have to like it. It's ironic: when your husband's away you teach yourself to be an independent person, yet because he's in the Army, you're never an independent person. You can't do what you want because you're part of the Army world. And when your husband comes home, you're even less independent then, because you have to play your part as his wife. If you go in the sergeants' mess, you're expected to join in with the other wives' talk: and it's always entirely Army, Army, Army. I sometimes feel like standing up and shouting "Don't you ever talk about anything else but the Army?" I'd love to see their faces in the mess if I did, because they don't think there's anything in life *but* the Army.

(Betty B., sergeant's wife)

— I don't think you can avoid the feeling if your husband's for instance a company commander, that you've also got a job, that of company commander's wife. It gives you a feeling of responsibility towards the wives who're married to the men he's in charge of. It's difficult to say precisely what I'm trying to say, but I sometimes have the feeling that I'm perhaps not devoting enough of my time to being part of a team with him. I don't know if wives of husbands in other jobs get that feeling. It sounds almost as though I'm suggesting that I work for the Army: which of course is ridiculous, not true, I don't. But there's a sort of moral pressure about it, I ought to do my best and put my part in John's job ahead of other things I might want to do.

(Laura M., major's wife)

— I find the snobbery among officers' wives particularly distasteful. I don't like it among the officers, but it's even more obnoxious when it's their wives. My husband worked his way up through the ranks, and he got to where he is now entirely by his own efforts. When some flouncy woman younger than me comes out with her la-di-da accent and she's saying — not using the exact words but very clearly implying it — "Your husband's done very well to get where he's got" — and her husband's only where he is because he's had the advantages of birth and education and family connections — well when that sort of woman starts patronizing me, I want to kick her shins good and hard for her.

(Maureen K., lieutenant's wife)

— I get bored rigid at the mess night dinners, I wonder how Geoffrey can stand working with such a lot of brainless ninnies as the others seem to be. They all only talk about the Army, the adventures they had on exercises, mutual acquaintances who got into situations which they think are uproariously funny and which to an outsider are completely dull. Their daft braying voices, I really could scream. I look round at their wives and I wonder how they can put up with these idiots who're their husbands. Then I think how my husband must look and sound to them, and perhaps how I must look and sound too. I know my husband isn't really like that underneath, he's acting the part of the Army officer when he's in among all the other Army officers. But when he's at home he's not like that, he's a warm and gentle human being. So I have to grant a lot of the others might be acting too. Why it's necessary for them I can't begin to imagine. Maybe it's a sort of defensive thing, the soldier defending himself against the outside world and not wanting to let his real personality show through. That's a thought I suppose, it'd never struck me before.

(Caroline C., captain's wife)

– I accept danger to him but I worry. When they were in Cyprus you only need to look at a map of the Mediterranean and see how close they were to some of the places in the Near East where there was fighting. You could see it could easily come about they might be caught up in something that they'd no idea of when they went there in the first place. So I accept the danger is part of his job, but it doesn't seem real to me because I'm not there when they're playing war. But I know their exercises are not really playing, they're more like rehearsing. I suppose if I knew he was engaged in real fighting I'd be much more worried. Northern Ireland was difficult when he went there on a short tour from Germany: it was only four months, but I knew he was in danger and it troubled me a lot. And I knew when I was honest with myself that not only was he in danger of being shot at, he was likely to be shooting at people himself too. I tried to blank that side of it out of my mind.

(Joyce L., corporal's wife)

– You can never imagine how much it's going to knock you sideways. You tell yourself your husband's in the Army, danger's part of it, and something might happen to him. The same as you must if your husband's on an oil rig or down a coal mine or in an aeroplane. But I hadn't been prepared for how I'd hear and what I'd do, and what effect it'd all have.

It was the lunchtime news on the radio when I first heard. They said there'd been a shooting incident involving some soldiers, and one soldier had been killed. This must sound snobbish: but when they said "soldier" it never crossed my mind it could be Philip. Then later on in the afternoon they referred to it again on the radio, this time they said an officer had been killed. It still didn't strike me it might be him, I took it for granted . . . well I'm not sure what I thought. I think I thought someone would come to the door or I'd have a phone call or something. Then the next thing I heard, I suppose it would've been on the six o'clock news, it said, "Next of kin have been informed." So it hardly interested me after that, I wasn't worried in any way.

About an hour later the phone rang and it was Philip's mother. She lives in the north, she often rang up from time to time for a chat. When I heard her voice I didn't think it was anything special, I said "Oh hello Mum, how are you?" She just said "Frances, oh Frances" that was all, just my name. Then I realized she was crying. And I thought she'd rung to tell me Dad had died: he'd been ill for some time. I said "It's all right, Mum, it's all right, tell me what's happened but don't worry now, take your time." I couldn't grasp what message she was trying to give me: and of course, she didn't know that I didn't know. So it was absolutely unreal and bizarre, the whole thing.

I didn't learn until quite a long time afterwards that the Army people had a note that I'd gone on holiday to my mother-in-law's, which I had. But I'd been back home a week, and they'd been trying to get in touch with me up there, I don't know all the ins and outs of it but there'd been a breakdown in communications somewhere.

So as I say that was how I heard. None of it seemed real, none of it was anything I could take in for several days. I'm still not sure what I feel about it. I have days when I get very angry, but I never know when they're going to happen. I wake up and start to feel the anger growing inside me against those people – people I don't know and never will know – who killed my husband. You need an object for hatred. Other days I feel angry about the Army: I know it was his job, but I feel angry they sent him on that particular operation instead of someone else. He'd been working under great pressure and strain, and it was always a big point with him that the most dangerous time was when you were tired, and your concentration started to slip. I'm still very very mixed up about it all.

(Frances P., lieutenant's wife)

16 In Ordinary Life

i. *Boxes: Harry Roberts,
    furniture dealer*

ii. *What I am now:
    Norman Jackson,
    stable manager*

iii. *Please God don't let it happen:
    Cathy Harper, secretary*

iv. *No sort of a job: Malcolm Grant,
    unemployed*

i. Boxes: Harry Roberts, furniture dealer

– Boxes. Look at me, here I am surrounded with them, all these tea chests: and I told myself when I left the Army I never wanted to see another one of their fucking boxes ever again. I sometimes felt as though I spent my whole life packing and unpacking the fucking things. You just get settled into your home, then it was off again: well a bit of an exaggeration, it was more every two years or so, but I know the wife hated them more than I did. And here we are now, and look: boxes, boxes, boxes. Funny the way life turns out sometimes, you have to laugh.

I came out after I'd done twelve, that was two years ago when I was thirty. I was a full corporal. It wasn't an easy decision and I didn't know what was going to happen to me. The gratuity I had wasn't princely, we had the two kids who were five and three, so we were taking a bit of a chance. It's not a great recommendation for a job of any sort to go to someone and tell them you've been in the Army twelve years. They look at you as though you must be a moron. One bloke I went to see about a job, he asked me straight out "What made you join the Army?" I don't know if he was expecting me to say "I fancied the idea of going round killing people," or what. But I told him straight: I said "I couldn't get any other job, and I'd always rather fancied it since I was a kid, but I couldn't tell you specially why." He didn't give me the job though.

Lots of other people didn't give me jobs either. I'm just trying to think of some of the things I tried for: sometimes I got interviews, most times I got nowhere as far as that. Van drivers for different sorts of firms, roundsman of one kind or another, office worker,

shop worker, security guard, trainee salesman flogging encyclo-
pedias. This list was pretty endless, and I didn't get a smell of any
of them, nowhere near. The Army doesn't prepare you for that, it
doesn't say if you go into civvy street you're likely to find it's a
handicap. They have a course you go on before you leave. It's not all
that helpful, but it does tell you a bit about starting up your own job.
That wasn't something I fancied myself: it was only over a year after
I'd been trying for everything suitable or unsuitable and got nowhere that I came round to thinking about the idea again. One day I
saw the ad in the paper for this second-hand furniture wholesale
business that was going. It was asking for the investment of a fair
amount of capital so I thought it'd be out of the question. But with a
bit of help from my parents, my wife's parents, one or two good
friends, and the bank manager, then I about managed to scrape up
enough to consider it. Then what did I do, well I got cold feet didn't
I? I thought I'll never make it, I'll never do it, I'm not a businessman,
I'll go bust in six months.

Perhaps I was at just the right time in the trade for coming in:
anyway it worked, or it has done all right so far. I go to houses and
buy their contents, or I go to auction sales and buy stuff in quantity.
It's not exactly high class antiques but it's not junk either. I've now
got a fair idea of the sort of things people want and what sort of
prices they'll pay. Basically you've got to know your customers:
mine are people with second-hand furniture shops. It's quite
interesting sometimes because you get fashions: suddenly everybody's after kitchen tables, or bedside tables, or chests or drawers. It
only seems to last a month or two, then they go off on to something
else. You never know why it started in the first place, you never
know why it drops off again: I have to take care not to get myself
overloaded with any particular type of thing.

– I don't know I could say anything I did in the Army prepared me
much for running my own business. I was a corporal in the officers'
mess, that's all. Apart from picking up how to serve at table and a
bit of stock-keeping, there wasn't much else turned out to be of use
for me. "Yes sir, no sir, three bags full sir" – that hasn't been any
help. As an NCO you take orders from your superiors, and you give
a few orders to those below you: but what that trains you for, except
to go on doing it for the rest of your life, it would be very hard to say.

One of the main benefits, I think it's the main benefit, is that the
wife and I are much happier now because we've got our own life and
we're not anybody's servants. We can decide to shut the shop on a

Saturday afternoon if we want to and go off in the car with the kids somewhere. There's no more me being sent away on exercises, or having to go abroad for four or six months. All that's gone and I don't regret that. It took us both time to get used to it, that we could actually please ourselves: when I look back on it now, I think in many ways the twelve years I had in the Army was twelve wasted years.

I remember one time not long after I'd joined as a young private, and we had a young Rupert, if you know that term, in charge of an exercise. He was "putting in an attack" as they say, and in his talk to us beforehand to give us extra confidence he said "Never forget if something goes wrong, it doesn't mean the attack has failed. You are replaceable, there'll always be others to come in your place." I thought "Marvellous, that's a fucking fine thing to be told: 'Don't worry if you get killed, we've got plenty more like you.'" I'd imagine that officer didn't get very far unless somebody took him in hand.

To me one of the weaknesses of the Army was definitely the officers. The Army couldn't exist without that kind of structure of superiors and inferiors which they have. It's not based on merit: and nobody objects to an officer who's earned his position the hard way, coming up from the ranks. But when you get some poncy young chap with a plum in his mouth who's only in the Army because he didn't have the initiative to go out and get himself a job, and he's in charge over you every minute of your day – he can get you into trouble whenever he feels like it, he can stop your money and stop your leave – those things like that, I think they're very wrong. I can tell you, since I've come out I've seen even more so how wrong they are. Life isn't like that outside, and pretending life is like that, which it is in the Army, isn't doing anyone a service.

They say the Infantry isn't as bad as some of the more snobbish regiments like the Guards and that lot, but believe me they could be pretty ridiculous at times. Some of those kids fresh from Sandhurst: I remember one one day complaining to me the water in the jug on the table wasn't cold enough, telling me to take it away and bring a replacement. What that's supposed to do for you I don't know, except feel like spitting in it before you put it back on the table.

Another thing they would do which was wrong was I got interested in the Army in playing rugby. I'd never played it before and I found out I was quite good at it. I was a regular in the battalion team. But when we had competitions that were knock-outs, say if there was an inter-battalion one, that had a lot of prestige to it. I was too good for them to do it to me, but there were others who weren't quite of the same standard: they'd be in the team right up to the semi-final, and then when we got to the final and it was going to be a bit of an occasion, when they put the team sheet up those blokes' names weren't on it. It was the officers who fancied themselves as rugby players who put themselves in the team just for the finals.

Some of them, they were so thick it was a joke. All right, it didn't matter if you were at home in England or had a cushy posting like Germany or Cyprus, but in somewhere say like Northern Ireland it was a different matter. If you found yourself going out on the streets with a young officer and you knew that he was no good at his job, it wasn't a good feeling. You thought "Christ, this guy could get me killed." I can't say I recollect an occasion where you could say definitely that mishandling by an officer brought a man to actually be killed, but in my own experience there were times when men weren't killed that wasn't due to the officer in charge. He would order you into situations where there was an element of risk without thinking it out properly: I'm talking now of when he'd order you to check a parked car. If you touched it there was a chance that you'd be blown to smithereens: it wasn't right men should be ordered to do that by officers trying to prove they were efficient. Of course you'd get the other sorts too, ones who'd say "Right Corporal, come with me, you and I are going to search that car." You'd think "Well you might want to be a fucking hero, sir, but I fucking don't." But you didn't have no choice about it.

I'm glad now that I'm out, and I wouldn't recommend anyone to go in. I was saying to you in the first talk we had that I couldn't think of anything the Army had trained me for: but I've been thinking about it since, and there is one thing that I ought to mention it did do for me. When I went in as an ordinary private, I was very very shy and didn't have much confidence in myself. Then when I started to go up through the different grades, lance corporal and then corporal – that did do a lot for me. The main thing was it gave me the confidence to talk to anyone. You learn to speak up for yourself, speak to other people without being frightened of them. That's a thing I got from the Army. But there was nothing else I'm particularly thankful for; and however hard it's been since, I'm still sure I did the right thing in coming out.

ii. What I am now: Norman Jackson, stable manager

– I'm forty-eight and I've been out of the Army six years. After twenty-two years I ended up as company sergeant major, and it'd been my intention to try and get on the Long Service List and stop in until I was in my fifties. But I was having poor health and the wife was keen for me to take things easy. Both our children were grown up and off our hands, and she felt after all the years I'd put in that the time had come for me to sit back and reap the benefit, living a quiet life on a not-too-bad pension.

It was a big decision and when we first talked it over I was all for it. But the nearer the time came for taking the actual step, the more I was hesitating in my mind about it. That was funny, because if there's one thing the Army teaches you it's not to dither. But I'd been in pretty well all my life, and it was the prospect of coming out into the world, I won't pretend anything different, it was downright scary. It wasn't the financial aspect, that was taken care of: in the last few years my wife had had a job herself, so we'd got our own house plus a bit put aside. The scary thing was in not knowing how I was going to cope and what I was going to do. I was the sort of person people would say had a khaki brain, I'd never thought of anything but Army.

What finally settled it was that our daughter who was married, she and her husband had their first baby and the wife wanted us to be near them. As I saw it I had to make my mind up, so I said to the wife, "Look, we can't go on like this: I'm definitely going to decide, and I'm going to decide now." I took a coin out of my pocket, and before she could say anything I flipped it up in the air and caught it, smacked it down on the back of my hand, took my other hand away and looked at it and said "Right that's it, I'm out of the Army." I hadn't told her whichever way it came up, that was what I was going to say. She stood there and she burst into tears. I thought "Oh Christ, I've said the wrong thing." But she flung her arms round my neck and kissed me, she said "Oh Norman, I'm so happy!" So it was OK.

For the first year or so I did nothing. I sat around in the house, I wore bedroom slippers all day, I read the newspapers and went to the pub at lunchtime for a drink, I had a nap in the afternoons – and all in all, I can tell you, I felt bloody awful. Time and again I thought to myself I'd made a terrible mistake. I just didn't know what to do with myself. We had a bit of a garden in the house we were living in, but I can't think of a single subject I'm less interested in than gardening unless it's possibly fruit machines. I tried: and every bloody thing I planted either didn't come up, or if it was a plant from a shop it withered and died. I've got black fingers you see.

The next thing I thought of doing was that I might set up a little business. I went down the town and looked around to get some ideas, but everything I looked at, none of them appealed to me. I couldn't see myself running a greengrocer's because that meant getting up early to go to the markets first thing in the morning: or a video rental shop, well everyone and his mother was running one of those. I had a relative who had a sweets and tobacconist, and I started looking for one of those in the trade papers. There was lots on offer, but I knew what this relative was earning out of his, and it seemed like a hell of a lot of work for very little money to me.

Whenever we talked about it the wife said "Look, just stay at home and enjoy yourself." I said "What, like counting the flowers on the wallpaper?" It was getting really bad. Then finally two things happened more or less at once. The first was I went to my GP and told him I was going crazy: I said I was going out of my mind with boredom, I wanted him to give me a complete check over to see how fit I was to do something. He fixed for me to go and see specialists as well, and at the end of it he said "For a man of your age you're 100 per cent." In other words, my health had improved and there was no reason for me to take things all that easy.

The other thing was that I saw in a local newspaper an advertisement at one of the racehorse establishments out on the edge of the town, saying they wanted a stable manager. I thought well I don't know much about horses, but I know about a few other things and it might be worth giving it a try. I'm not a great one for letter writing, so I was cheeky, I rang them up and said I was interested, could I go and see them, and they said Yes.

When I got there, I found my hunch had been right. They'd apparently had a bad experience with somebody who'd been with them for several years: he'd been given a free hand on the administration side, and to coin a phrase he'd been taking them for a ride. A few hundred quid here, another few hundred there: he'd got quite a nice little racket running with two or three other members of the establishment. So what they were chiefly looking for was really an administrator: somebody who they could rely on as utterly honest and reliable, and who could generally organize things so that side of it didn't need to cause any problems. It meant such things as supervising the cash for the wages, not actually doing the books but making sure they were done, running what they call the diaries, and all that sort of thing. Apart from the fact it was to do with horses rather than men, it was more or less what I'd been doing during my last years in the Army. I said to the owner, who incidentally is Sir Somebody Somebody, "I don't see what you've got to lose by giving me a chance sir. If you want somebody who can run a good organization, who's utterly trustworthy, and who'll give you absolute loyalty – well, you'd have to go a long way to find somebody better than me." I was very modest you see. So he said to me "Well, so long as you don't behave like a bloody sergeant major and have everybody doing things at the double and standing to attention, you sound like the sort of person I want." I said to him "Give me a chance to show you sir," and he did.

There's this public stereotype of the sergeant major, I think people get it from the television. So it wasn't difficult for me to show him even in the first couple of days that I didn't operate that way. I think he was pleased with me, I've been with him three years up to now, we've never had the slightest little thing go wrong, and what's more we've not had a single person on the staff who's asked to leave. So that tells you something.

The trouble with a lot of soldiers, particularly if they've got on in the Army and up in the ranks to senior NCOs, they feel they can walk into any job in civvy street then, and people are waiting to welcome them with open arms. It's not true, I was one of the very lucky ones in getting into the first job I tried for. But you can see in what that man said to me, a lot of civilian people have a fixed idea in their mind about what they're going to find if they take on an ex-soldier. They're wrong but since they're the people in the position to offer you the job, their idea of an ex-Army man can work against you. Once you've got in you can prove to them they were wrong like I did: but in a lot of cases you won't even get in because of the prejudice. I'd say to any soldier who comes out that he should bear it in mind: the qualities that got him on in the Army could be the very ones to make him unsuitable for civvy street.

My son is twenty now and at university. He comes up against this too. Sometimes he'll bring someone home, then afterwards he says "My girlfriend said you weren't anything like she expected when I told her my Dad was an ex-Army sergeant major." You can't blame the girl, that's what she's been fed on in the newspapers and on the telly. I read a book in the library the other day about a group of soldiers in Northern Ireland: a fiction book, a story, and the sergeant in charge was a downright bully. What I'm saying is not there aren't bullies among sergeant majors in the Army, but there are plenty who aren't. Anyone reading that book, the writer was playing in with what his readers expected.

I'm not hoping my boy goes in the Army: he's a brain boffin, a very clever lad, we're very proud of him. He's getting a much better education than I ever had, and I hope he's going to make something of his life. Civil engineering is his particular line, and I think he'll go a long way in it, much further than he could ever get in the Army.

The Army does to a certain extent tend to make you into one amongst thousands in a big institution: but you don't have to make your children follow along the same way. It does lead people to being institutionalized, there's no doubt about that. When I was in the Army coming up the ranks, I liked to know what was what and who was where at any particular time of day. It makes me blush to talk about it now, but I used to pin a sheet of paper on the back of the kitchen door when I was on leave, giving information for the kids about the forthcoming week: where we were going, what time we were setting off, and even our meal times. My wife started doing it too, originally to humour me: but then she found her life was easier to cope with if she followed the same method. When I came out, that was one of the first things I told myself I wasn't going to do any more, all that sort of business was over and done with. But my wife went on doing it, she said she was used to it, it worked, and she liked to know where she was even if I didn't. We had a real laugh about it: I said to her "If it's the last thing I do, I'm going to demilitarize you!" Finally she stopped doing it, but it took time.

Summing up I'd say the Army had done me a lot of good, it provided me with a lot of happy times as well as difficult times. I don't regret any of it, but now I'm away from it I'm glad I'm leading what you might call a second life. It's only now that I've come to realize what I am now, just another ordinary human being who can take pleasure in doing a job and doing it well: living very happily with his wife, and watching their children grow up and make their own futures.

iii.   Please God don't let it happen: Cathy Harper, secretary

– No, I don't mind talking to you about it. He died six years ago, I've recently remarried, my second husband and I've no secrets between us. He's trying to be, and so far's made a very good job of being, a father to my daughter, Emma. She was nine then, fifteen now: I was thirty-six then, I'm forty-two now.

We married when I was twenty, and at that time Bob'd only just joined the Army. I'd never thought I'd be married to a soldier, I didn't come from an Army background: nor did he, he was just an ordinary boy from the next village to where I lived in Bedfordshire. We met one night at a friend's twenty-first birthday party. He'd just signed up: and the usual thing, we wrote to each other and found we liked each other. When he had to go away we found the separation had brought us closer together in a way when he came back. Then the time came when he was going to be posted to Germany and he asked me to marry him and I said I would. On the whole I think we had a quite happy time. I didn't like being an Army wife, but I knew what I was taking on when we got married and I accepted it. I think it's inevitable there were times, I think everyone feels it, that I felt the Army occupied more of his life than I did.

Especially after Emma was born I found that really I was the one who had nearly all the upbringing of her. Bob was ambitious, he wanted to get on, and I knew he really had no choice about where he was sent and when. He really didn't have choice: he was sent, and I think a lot of Army wives didn't always appreciate that. Some of them seemed to have a sneaking feeling at the back of their minds that their husbands didn't have to go away quite so often as they made out, and could do something about it if they complained. We had our separations, but we had times too when we went to say Germany or Northern Ireland on fairly long tours of duty, and we settled there and made the place our home wherever we were. Even when we went to Northern Ireland, I was much happier when Emma and I could be there with him than when for instance we were in Germany, and he was sent off to Ireland for short periods and we couldn't go.

Bob was never particularly a warlike man, and as far as I know he wasn't ever involved in much in the way of fighting: he never talked about it, so I don't really know if he was or not. It was something I made a conscious effort to put out of my mind: either people trying to kill him, or him perhaps defending himself and killing others. I don't think either happened: I like to think it didn't. In ordinary life you never think about that sort of thing because you don't have to. It's funny I say "in ordinary life" . . . I suppose it shows how much I've now moved away from the Army. But at the time there didn't seem to be any other life: it had a lot of benefits I was grateful for like the security, the pleasure in going to places, the pleasure I got from knowing he was doing something he really liked. Very often wives feel, don't they, their husband is just doing his job to provide for them and the children? I never had to feel that with Bob. I knew if he really hated it he could give it up if he wanted to. I don't mean immediately, but no one has to stay in the Army if they don't like it. But he did like it: liked the variety, he was always saying he was glad he didn't have a boring job in a factory or something like that.

The main problem of course was schools for Emma. We moved around, no more than anyone else did but it was unsettling and confusing for her. I don't think she minded the different quarters we lived in, because she was with me and her father, but it was difficult about schools. I read somewhere once that in the American Army, wherever they are their schools use the same syllabus and the same textbooks. So that way, if soldiers' children move from one place to another they don't have to make a lot of adjustment. But with Emma she was always finding herself either behind her class or sometimes in front of it: or having to use different books and all the rest of it. It must have been hard for her, and it didn't give her much chance to make friends because she was being constantly up-rooted. The Army does a lot for families, but I think that's one area where they fall down. Sometimes Emma went to a local school: in

Northern Ireland for instance, and she felt very much out of it there.

I was saying Bob wasn't really a fighting man. He was in the stores: like everyone else he had to do his training for fighting, but I used to think wherever they went he'd be comparatively safe. There was a time once when he got the chance of more rapid promotion when he was offered a different job: I don't understand the mechanics of it, but his commanding officer told him if he transferred into a different company and did a job that involved fighting, he'd find himself getting promotion much more quickly. I used to pray about it. I knew in the end Bob would do what he was told, and if he was told to go into the other company he'd have no choice about it. I used to pray "Please God don't let it happen." Well perhaps there's something in praying, because it didn't.

I'd certainly have prayed if I'd ever known he was in danger or in action, but I knew he wasn't. So him dying came as a terrible shock to me. It was just about the furthest thing from my mind that anything like it could happen. He was in Northern Ireland: we all were, we were living there, and then there was this accident with a truck and he was killed. He was a war casualty, but you couldn't put the blame on any enemy of any kind, because his death was a result of something that happened on his own side and didn't have anything to do with anyone else.

It was a very difficult thing to try to explain to Emma. I'd told her since she was very little that her Daddy was a soldier, he might one day be in a war, and that one day something might happen to him. I didn't build him up to her as anything special, but I did say he was a brave man who was prepared to give his life to protect his own country. I suppose in a way it would have been an easier thing to explain to her if it had happened like that. But to say her Daddy had been killed in an accident, well I found that very hard. So did she too, and I know it's still on her mind because she sometimes brings it up. She's fifteen now and can understand things much better. Only the other day she said very quietly and sadly when there was something on the television news about the Army, "I wish my Dad hadn't been a soldier." Perhaps it's better though that she shouldn't have false ideas about him dying a hero's death. He wouldn't have liked that himself. They say time heals, but I do find it very hard to talk about it still even now. I'm sorry.

– The Army treated me well after his death, and I get the pension. They were not very good when it first happened, everything took ages to come through, but that was bad organization rather than anything else. I first heard when his company commander came round to our quarter to see me: he must have thought I'd already been told, because when I opened the front door he was standing there and took his cap off. Nobody had been to tell me anything, but I knew from that gesture he'd brought some very bad news. I asked him in, and took him into the sitting room, then I turned round and said "What is it, what's happened?" He said "I'm terribly sorry about it." I said "About what?" When it dawned on him this was the first I'd heard of it, he went red in the face and got very angry. He started saying it was disgusting, I could rest assured that he'd kick up a stink about it when he got back that I hadn't been properly told. I suppose he was embarrassed to find himself in that position. I wasn't all that worried about the embarrassment, I was more or less in a state of shock at obviously what he was telling me or thought he was telling me. I really couldn't have cared whether anybody got into trouble or not. That was a very awkward few minutes for him and for me. But now as I say, all of it seems a long time ago. I'm still young enough to have a future to look forward to, and to hope Emma will grow up in a settled home with me and her stepfather. We've talked about having another child but decided against it for her sake, I think it would cause too many problems all round.

The years I was a soldier's wife, I look back on them as sixteen years out of my life that went for nothing. It doesn't make me bitter, he could have had an accident even if he hadn't been in the Army. I used to get invited to reunions and things, but I never went: and since I remarried, obviously I wouldn't want to. I met a man a few years back, he'd been one of Bob's Army friends and he said to me "Ah the good old days Cathy, I often think of them." I said "Do you? I don't." It was true. The Army means nothing to me now.

iv.   No sort of a job:
Malcolm Grant, unemployed

– I came out a year ago when I was aged twenty-nine, and so far I haven't been able to find any work at all of any kind. No sort of a job: I'm one of the massed ranks of the unemployed.

I came out with the rank of lieutenant, after ten years in the Infantry. I don't come from an Army family, it was entirely my own choice that after "A" levels I should go to Sandhurst. I'm very bored because I can't get work, and in a sense I think the Army can be very very restrictive on one's outlook. As an officer you lead a very cosseted sort of life, so when you make the break and come out, you have a hell of a problem. At least I myself had a hell of a problem trying to fit into the world outside. When you've been spending your days and nights almost entirely with men mostly of your own age, who never talk of anything else but Army, you only need go into a pub and listen to people talking to realize what few subjects of conversation you've picked up yourself.

I'd reached the point when I either had to sign on again and commit myself for the next decade of my life at least, even if I only did it bit by bit, or I had to break away. I didn't talk to my parents about joining the Army, so I didn't go and talk with them about leaving either. There was a girl involved, in fact it was on the cards we'd get married: but when I asked her if she'd marry me if I came out of the Army, her enthusiasm for the idea seemed to go into a rapid decline. I think she liked the idea of being married to an Army officer rather more than she liked the idea of being married to me as a person. That sounds like a sour thing to say, but all the same after we broke off our engagement in about three months she became engaged to one of my friends who's still an Army officer.

Because we don't have conscription and all soldiers are volunteers rather than pressed men, the Army considers itself to be an elite. They stress the concept of being professional, whatever that means. And as well as feeling that about itself, its officers consider themselves to be an elite within an elite – socially, intellectually, morally and in every other way. They really do think they're superior to other people. It's because they spend their lives with people below them obeying their every – well, I was going to say "command", but it's more than that – it's their every whim. In the mess they don't have to help themselves to their drinks, lower breeds bring it for them. They don't have to keep their rooms clean, other lower breeds – women in this case – are employed to clean and tidy them up. It may well suit the Army to have that system, but it's a really lousy preparation for living outside. I've sometimes thought looking back on it that it's part of a way of making sure you're not fitted to living outside. So this'll put extra pressure on you to stay in, because they want you to after all the money they've spent on training you.

I'd say that if you want comparative ease and security in life, and you don't come from a family who can afford to give it you, then the Army's quite a good option. But nothing comes free, and so there're things you have to sacrifice in return. For a start, your independence, because the Army owns you body and mind. It might not be so bad if you sold them only the body part, but you can't get away with that. You simply can't afford, not if you're career-minded, to be in the slightest way non-conformist or even be suspected of being that way. You have to accept all their values without exception. In the mess there's a fresh supply of newspapers every day: but it's the unusual or exceptional mess which will take even such a paper as the *Guardian*. That's considered radical and left wing. Similarly with magazines, I've never seen a mess in which you'd find the *New Statesman*. The point I'm making is that officers are mostly the kind of unthinking Tories who consider themselves non-political. That means they're fundamentally extremely right-wing Conservative.

Another thing is the Army says, every time the subject's raised, that snobbery in the Army is much less than it used to be. If that's the case I shudder to think what it was like before my time. The Army perpetuates the British class system, and it couldn't exist in its present form without that class system. It has to have the acceptance, without thinking or questioning let alone challenging it, by some men that they're only fit to be inferiors: with the corollary, the assumption by others that they're in some way chosen by God as superiors.

They'll tell you too that there's no obstacle to people from non-public school backgrounds becoming officers. Nor is there: but you'll notice in the mess that those like that are treated slightly patronizingly by the others. When you've come up through the ranks, if you do get a commission there's only a certain number of jobs you stand any chance of getting: Families Officer, Assistant Adjutant, Quartermaster – and a few more, and they're all that's open to you. You'll never get one of the plum jobs. It's for your satisfaction, so you can look back and pat yourself on the back about how far you've got: but there's a limit to how far you get in status as an officer. And yet the biggest snobs in fact are those officers who've come up from the ranks: they're worse than anybody towards the ordinary soldiers, and about the traditions of the mess: people wearing ties and all that kind of thing. They defend it on the grounds they're "maintaining standards" – but they're the standards of one class of society, which wasn't even originally their own.

I found an air of unrealism in a lot of other areas too. Training, for instance: you'd have an exercise in which the task you were given was to attack or defend a certain point, all played out with complete seriousness. The assumption was the enemy in the next war was going to abide by the rules of the last war or possibly even the one before that. I read a book which criticized the French army for basing most of its training before the 1939–45 war on cavalry movements, and largely ignoring tanks. What you've got now almost entirely throughout the British Army is training based on infantry attacks and tank movements. The concept that war is never going to be like that again, that it'll be fought with nuclear weapons in which not just soldiers but whole populations will be obliterated, well that's something which hasn't penetrated. If it had of course you wouldn't be able to have exercises. There are now and again a few in which everyone runs round in so-called "anti-nuclear" gear, but it's ludicrously inadequate. The Army just blindly hopes the next war will be fought in the same way as the last one. But try and start a discussion in the mess on the subject and question these assumptions, and you're looked upon as a Bolshie. They don't want to think about it, let alone talk about it.

In this sense the Falklands war was a disaster. It only reinforced old-fashioned notions of how wars could be fought. You only need ask yourself how we'd have behaved if it had been the Russians who had occupied the islands. We certainly wouldn't have sent off our glorious task force: we'd have gone running to the negotiating table, proving once and for all that warfare of that kind is out of date.

Another example to me of the outmoded ideas in the Army was the subject of homosexuality. Whisper it quietly, but more than one famous Army figure of the past has been, as we're now slowly learning from time to time, homosexual. But the official line within the Army in present day terms is that it doesn't exist. You put a whole lot of men together, in parlous conditions sometimes in a foreign country – and all you offer them in the way of sex is brothels or the local prostitutes. At the first suggestion of homosexual behaviour between any of the men, they're thrown out. The Army not only doesn't condone homosexuality – and incidentally I think I'm right in saying you can no longer be given the sack in outside society simply for being homosexual – it not only doesn't condone it, it closes its eyes and goes blue in the face and swears it doesn't exist. I've known more than a few soldiers who've been turfed out for homosexual behaviour. I think most people nowadays would agree that a man's sexual inclinations have nothing to do with his qualities as a soldier. This is something I think the Army certainly needs to bring itself into the twentieth century about.

I'd say the time I spent in the Army was, for me personally, a mistake. I didn't fit, and I realized it, and I got out. Obviously I feel it didn't do me a lot of good: obviously I feel, because I've had no success in getting work since, that it really wasn't any help to me in later life. I don't want to give the impression that I didn't enjoy my time: I did, there were lots of interesting and exciting times, and I made some good friends. But I wasn't meant for the Army perhaps, and the Army wasn't meant for me. It's been – I can't think of any other way to put it – it's been in a way like a divorce. Like a divorce, it's a painful and slow process, with in some respects some blows to one's own self-esteem. You see the Army doesn't help you to know yourself: it teaches you to subjugate yourself and your own personality to something much bigger, which is why it can't cope with non-conformists. In a way it brainwashes you: you not only wear uniform, but you are and you have to be mentally in uniform yourself. There's no margin for moving outside clearly defined limits: if you want to, and you do, you find yourself in a position where you must leave if you're to survive as a person.

17   Coda: The Sweet War Man

You've known since we first met that I'm a pacifist, that I was a conscientious objector in World War II, and would be one again if that sort of situation ever recurred. Not to argue or debate the subject – but would you tell me something about your own beliefs, about the conscience of a soldier?

– Well, I think people like you who are pacifists are totally unrealistic. During my service in different parts of the world I've met people who could only be described as pathological killers, who enjoy fighting and killing. In some cases like the IRA they're a small but very dangerous minority of people in a society: but in others, where their leaders have what one might almost call a Messianic flavour and whip people up to follow them, it really would be completely ludicrous to stand aside if one was threatened by them, and offer them no resistance.

I've no doubt that I have a moral right – indeed I've no doubt that I have a moral duty – to protect wife, family, other people's wives and families, my society, and my country, from people like that. I have a degree of admiration for those who follow the Christian principles of forgiveness extended to all, but I also am a Christian believer. I think when lives are in danger and one's country's whole way of life is under threat, it's unreasonable and, if you'll forgive me, naive not to be prepared to fight to defend it. You will get yourself killed, you will allow your family and friends to be killed: and you will achieve nothing. I think I'd almost go further and say it could be argued that that attitude was immoral: one has the right to allow one's own life to be taken, but does one have the right to allow

others to lose their lives, without trying to do a thing to save
them?

                                    (*Richard J., commanding officer*)

– Where I think you're completely wrong is you imagine the rest of
the world's like you. Believe me mate it fucking isn't. The world's
full of fucking lunatics, who'd kill you and take your home and
everything soon as look at you. If you was living in some other
country, and I could name you half a dozen because I've been in
them, you'd have a much clearer idea then of what life was really all
about. Life's about survival, for yourself and your family. How can
someone like you, coming from the sort of background you do, have
any idea at all? I've seen people killing other people just so's
they could get enough to eat for themselves: there wasn't enough
food, and they were determined they were going to have it to live
on. Or I've been in countries where people kill one another –
and their families and their children too – for religious reasons,
because they happen to be of a different faith. Are we going to say
we're just going to sit on our backside and let that sort of thing
happen?

    You see, not being personal about it, but you and people like you
leave all the dirty work to people like me, while you reap the benefit.
"Oh no" you say, "I couldn't soil my hands with anything like
that." Well it's all right for you to have that sort of an idea, because
you live in a country where you live in a society that people like me
are prepared to lay down our lives for.

                                                (*Jack. R., sergeant*)

– My husband would be prepared to give his life to protect me and
my children, and you and your children. That's what he's commit-
ted himself to do and what he's prepared to do: and it's what I'd
expect him to do if he was called upon. It's a way of life that asks him
to make sacrifices on your behalf, on everybody's behalf who lives
in the same society. He's prepared to do it, I'm prepared for him to
do it. God knows no one could hope harder than I do that he'd never
have to risk his life: I don't want a dead hero for a husband, I'd
sooner have a live coward. But it honestly seems to me you have to
have certain things you're prepared to die for, and if you haven't I
think you have to ask yourself how your conscience permits you to
allow other people to do it on your behalf.

                                            (*Sheila P., corporal's wife*)

– I feel it's morally right to be a soldier, and by that I mean being an extension of the political will of my country. It often means what we're doing is risking our lives buying time for politicians to sort things out. But because we're an elective democracy, they have a mandate. In some senses I feel we're similar to civil servants, in that we carry out the wishes of our masters. I've no feelings of compunction about what we do at all: if that's the choice of politicians, we're there as their servants. I'd even go so far as to say we don't necessarily have to agree with them, again drawing the comparison with civil servants who don't make policy but carry it out. I've served about half my time under a Labour government and the other half under a Conservative one. I happen to vote Labour, but I'd still have been ready to go and fight in the Falklands even though I disagreed with the Conservative government in the matter.

We're trained to do a job, to go to war, if necessary to kill people. We hope it'll never happen, but if it does we're ready and we'll go and we'll fight, and we'll kill and we'll be killed. But we're not automatons about it: we reckon we're peace-keepers more so than someone like you who talks vaguely about the virtues of peace but doesn't actually do anything to preserve it. When trouble breaks out anywhere in the world, I'm one of the thousands who'll go there to try and calm things down – the fire-fighter, if you like. But what do you do? You just sit at home and say "Oh how shocking." I'm not saying it's hypocritical or anything like that, I'm just saying we have a totally different way of looking at things. I suppose you would argue you can't keep peace by making war: but I'd argue the exact opposite, that if you're not ready if necessary to make war, you'll never keep the peace.

(David J., lieutenant)

– To be a soldier can be regarded by other people as quite unjustifiable. Taking up arms against one's fellow men, being prepared to kill them because they have an opposing or different point of view . . . it is, it's hard to justify that. You'll have heard it said we're the tool of politicians, they demand of us we should do what they say. They would even use us against the civilian population if it was a question of maintaining law and order and keeping themselves in power. So you have to think about these things and consider what sort of a person you are or could become. As a deliberate policy in my life I've tried to make as many friends as I could who are not soldiers, because I'm very anxious I shouldn't ever become a completely unthinking one. My wife and I have friends, or at least we could call them acquaintances, who while they're not actually pacifists sometimes give us the impression they think my job is a rather immoral one, the sort they wouldn't like to be involved with themselves.

I find this hurtful of course. Soldiers are often accused of talking and behaving as though they felt themselves to be some kind of elite. And I find that very distasteful, I don't like to hear such suggestions. But it's not greatly different to suggestions the other way, that if you're a soldier you're some kind of pariah, some kind of moral outcast. It's been very interesting to have a lifetime pacifist among us on so many occasions, for such a length of time, and in so many places. I think it's right that soldiers of all ranks and types should mix with people who are not soldiers and who never could be. I hope also that the experience has been of some value to you, and that we've both learned something from each other.

(Peter M., commanding officer)

– If you was never in the Army or wanted to be, then I would say I was sorry for you, because you've missed out on a great life. There's friends, going to different countries, sport, all the things that make the Army what it is. And if the reason was because you didn't agree with fighting, then I'd say I was even more sorry for you, because to my mind you would have to be a very peculiar sort of person. A man who won't stand up and fight when he has to is a strange kind of man, and I think most people would agree with that. I wouldn't say it was cowardice or anything, just that it was a funny way of looking at things. I mean if you don't fight, you never get nowhere: and it's the same whether you're a school kid in a playground, or a football team, or a country, or anything. Everyone fights for what they believe in, and if they don't they can't really believe in anything much. Or at least that's the way I see it.

(Andy C., private)

– It might sound a totally ridiculous thing for me to say, but I completely agree with you. I think war is very wrong: and any country which indulges in it, unless its borders are invaded, is usually to some degree at least in the wrong. As an instrument of policy, as a method, I think it's quite appalling to be prepared to try and kill as many of the enemy as possible, including the civilian population, men, women, children, the old, the aged, the infirm. The whole idea of slaughtering them until they give in is dreadful. The apotheosis of war to me was the Americans' use of the atomic bomb: and let's not forget they're the only people so far who have ever used such frightful weapons. There was no pretence about what they were trying to do at Hiroshima and Nagasaki, they were trying to obliterate them and every single living soul in them. It can't be justified, nor can the threat of doing it be justified on the grounds of deterrence. It's a completely, totally, inhumane action. The only logical and morally correct thing one can do is say "I'll have no part in it," and by progression "I'll have no part in saturation bombing such as Dresden, I'll have no part in all-out warfare in which civilians and their homes are destroyed." And so on and so on until one reaches the point of saying, "Not only will I not take part in organized warfare, but I will not kill my neighbour, and most certainly not try to hurt my neighbour by killing his wife and his children."

To me this is the logical pacifist position. Although I don't know if you agree with this, I suspect that people like you are saying that humankind has to find some other, different way of settling its quarrels because killing one another is never justified: and the fact that other people do it has nothing whatsoever to do with it. It's a matter for the individual conscience, for each individual to work out how far he's prepared to go. I respect that and I accept it as a perfectly correct and justifiable moral point of view.

Having said that, I sit here in my uniform and say that in my job as a soldier I would do what was required of me as a soldier. I hope I don't sound too utterly cynical and without principle when I say thousands of other people like me do things in their job which they feel, if they had to appear in front of a tribunal and justify, they could never do it. I wouldn't even want to plead, if any such occasion arose, that I was only carrying out orders. This doesn't release me from the responsibility for my own actions, finally.

I'm not arguing I'm a hypocrite without principles, I'm arguing I'm acting in our society as most people act – doing things which they don't agree with at all. But – and this is the crunch point my friend – they feel that with society being as it is, there's no other realistic alternative. You have to do things in every walk of life which you know in your heart of hearts are wrong. Your society in which you live, you know in your heart of hearts it's got many things wrong with it. But you are a member of it, and that's why you act as you do. No one is a free agent who can cut himself off from society and say it's nothing to do with him: everyone bears responsibility for the actions of the whole of society. Me as a soldier, you as a conchie – we're both in society and both responsible to a degree for what our society does and how it behaves.

(*Charles T., sergeant major*)

– My experience of soldiers at every level is that they have a strong conscience: I'm amazed at their broadmindedness and general kindness and courtesy and sense of humour. These things come out particularly in their handling of relationships with civilians. Even in riot situations they're amazingly restrained: rampant violence is not a sensible way to proceed in response to a difficult situation, and it's not the first instinct of a British soldier ever to apply overt aggression. They'll fight but they're not going out looking for a fight.

Those who so abhor violence of any kind that they conscientiously object to serving in any form that might lead them to kill – well, my judgment would be there'll always be some like that. But male human instinct being to defend oneself physically, there'll never be a lot. We have to have a system to ensure those who are conscientious objectors are genuine, and we have to say to them, "Right, well you do not need to carry arms." My instinct would be that people like that should serve without weapons and be put for instance into the medical sections, or as drivers or something like that. They would have to prove their case very thoroughly to a board of some kind though.

I think a problem arises when one sees these young people in big 'peace' demonstrations. Rightly or wrongly, they have a strong feeling that things are not right, and I would agree that we must address this matter. It's a political matter, but it must be addressed: we must come to a mutual understanding of why we need to have armed forces, why we need to have nuclear weapons: and the dialogue's a very important one. The young, who've always by the way been against force, have always too been the brightest of idealists. But they must be encouraged to listen to the alternative view, though that doesn't mean they're expected to agree. Indeed they may be right: and if they are we must come to terms with that. I personally don't believe they are right – but that's why I think there should be a dialogue with them in which they're encouraged to listen as well as to speak.

At the moment I think far too many of them don't listen: they just want to parade their idealism. That's not a virtue, it's actually the opposite, it's blindness. The dialogue has to be politically led, but in the best sense politically: by that I mean by politicians who're of high integrity, and who speak out expressing the need for armed forces, expressing the threat that society faces because that's the only justification for applying the money and resources to armed forces.

As for certain soldiers you tell me you've met who're members of CND, it's my view they can perfectly well understand the subject of nuclear arms and nuclear disarmament without being members of CND. That's to provide CND with unnecessary and ill-justified encouragement: and I think if a soldier feels like that, he should examine his conscience very carefully and if need be get out of the Army. I take a pretty adverse view of CND. I believe there are some who are idealistic and very fine people, but unfortunately it's become a vehicle for others whose attitudes and aims are rather more suspect. I've no direct evidence for this, I can only observe from a distance, but I think it would be very dangerous for soldiers formally to be members of CND.

However, that said, I do believe nuclear weapons are abhorrent. They are indiscriminate, and their only justification is to deter others from using them. But I believe they are essential until we have guarantees that are totally cast iron about other people's intentions. What saddens me is I think we're not going to get those guarantees, so we're going to need to continue to have nuclear weapons. This is a practical idealist speaking: I would love there to be no nuclear weapons, it would quieten the minds of millions: but I fear we can't trust those organizations which are our potential adversaries.

(Sir David Thorne, General)

– The Army to me is like an island in a sea of people. It's surrounded by all sorts of tides and currents: sometimes they're pleasant and balmy, sometimes they're rough and stormy. But we are the people's Army, we're there to do what their leaders order us to do. I know this was one of the strongest charges levelled against the German soldiers, that they tried to excuse what they'd done by saying they were obeying orders. They didn't know those orders were illegal: and what should they have done anyway, they'd have been shot if they'd refused? It isn't really a soldier's fault if he does things which are illegal: the people who ought to be the scapegoats, if there are to be any, should be the people who gave the orders.

This is rather wandering off the point of pacifism though isn't it? I'd say of myself that basically I'm as pacific a person as you are. But I have my ideas and my ideals, and one of them is that if it becomes necessary to fight in defence of the country or our way of life, I'm trained to do it, I'm amongst the first who'd be called on, and I'd hope I'd be amongst the first who'd step forward to do it. You might think this is very wrong. But I don't, I think it's justified and I think one adjusts oneself to the world as one sees it. I see it as in some places and some instances a dangerous and threatening place. I feel this view is borne out historically. Over the last two or three decades our politicians have given away – well that's not the right phrase, you can't give away something which isn't yours in the first place – let me put it this way, our politicians have restored independence to people all over the world. I don't think you could quote me one place where the British Army has invaded and taken over: at worst we've sometimes been slow at withdrawing, but there's nowhere we've conquered, not in my lifetime at least.

(*Adrian A., second lieutenant*)

– I think by and large you do have to question yourself about this at some stage in your career, and the earlier you do it the better. I don't know if you've seen the glossy brochure the Army gives people who inquire about becoming Army officers? One of its very early pages is a close-up photo of a hand holding a rifle with a finger on the trigger, and underneath it says "Could you give the order to fire?" Then it goes on in the text opposite to discuss the moral issue, and sets out clearly what it is: defending democracy and being prepared to use force to do it.

This is something you have to sort out, this issue in your own conscience: whether it's right or wrong actually to take life, or be prepared to take life, for the principles you believe in. Any soldier who hasn't thought this out and made a decision for himself is not going to be a good soldier. He should most definitely think about it. In my case, when I decided to join the Army I was probably about the same age you were when you decided to become a conscientious objector, in my late teens or early twenties. But what made you make your decision and me mine . . . well, that's probably something only a psychiatrist could tell us.

(*Jim S., major*)

– Soldiering too is a matter of conscience to a very great degree. You feel you've chosen to be a defender in the case of an attack on the state. And you feel you have the right actually to go as far, if necessary, to kill. But as I've said in previous talks, soldiers are not pathological killers. And we don't encourage them to behave as though they were, unless and until it's absolutely necessary. Then we encourage them to become psyched up so they're ready both to kill or be killed. In some armies I've visited it's thought to be manly simply to kill. But this doesn't occur in our Army: you'll never be introduced to somebody on the grounds that he's one of our leading slaughtermen.

No soldier glories in war. It's an awful and terrible business. So you have to think it through for yourself, you have to ask yourself "Is what I am doing justifiable, is what I'm prepared to do justifiable?" Killing happens very rarely, but it does happen: you wouldn't be a realistic soldier if you didn't accept that. When you open fire, or when you order your men to open fire, you don't see the end of the bullet's path. You don't know whether it hits a wall and drops expended and harmless, whether it ends in somebody's body. If it does you hope it will be one of the armed fighters on the other side: but you also have to accept it could cause the death of somebody not directly involved in the fighting.

I don't want to take the analogy too far, but violence is a tool which you use to achieve an objective or an end. One can think of other spheres of activity in which violence is used in a similar way: but with us it's our trade, our profession, and we're prepared to use it in that way. But I don't think most of us are by nature particularly violent men.

(Tom S., lieutenant)

Acknowledgments

As said, the original idea for this book came from Charles Clark: thereafter, I became indebted to many many people, to whom I owe profound thanks for making it possible for me to do it.

Brigadier David Ramsbottom and Derek Knight at the Ministry of Defence opened doors and smoothed my path and passed me on to HQ Eastern District; and there it was my very great good fortune to find myself in the hands of Reg Peachey and Major Tim Wakefield. They were unendingly and unreservedly friendly, efficient and imaginative in their responses to every single one of my requests: and it's no exaggeration to say not only that without their enthusiastic and unfailing co-operation and assistance the book would never have been completed, but also that without them I should not have enjoyed doing it to anything like the same extent that I truly did. I hope with both of them to continue the friendship we formed for a long time to come.

Most – but not all – the soldiers I met through them, and visited and talked with in various countries and places, were Royal Anglians, members of the 1st, 2nd and 3rd Battalions: The Vikings, The Poachers and The Pompadours. All three of their respective commanding officers, Lieutenant Colonel Tony Calder, Lieutenant Colonel Julian Browne and Lieutenant Colonel Alan Thompson, gave me the warmest hospitality and the greatest helpfulness whenever and wherever I visited them, despite all their other pressures of work. Three men in particular took on the responsibility of arranging time-schedules and interviews and introductions for me: they were Major Peter Ferrary, Major Guy Hipkin and Major Mike Menage. Without exception they looked after me, answered my endless questions, and never allowed me to feel other than always and entirely welcome. I must warmly thank too General Sir David Thorne and his wife Lady Anne for their friendliness and hospitality when I stayed with them for a few days in Germany.

I travelled in all about 28,000 miles to visit soldiers and their wives; I tape-recorded interviews with 181 people, often five or six times each, and talked with over a hundred more at some length. Every single name but one has been changed, and all identities have been obscured or concealed. This was not my original intention before I began the book: but requests for me to do so were so frequent, so strong, and became so regular and insistent that I eventually decided it was the only possible way to proceed. What was said, however, has not been altered in any way whatsoever: the book is a true record of the words of soldiers and their wives, and I am deeply grateful to them for speaking as forthrightly as they did and trusting me with their thoughts and feelings and ideas. I should also add that if there are any mistakes in terminology they must be blamed entirely on my own inability to hear, or properly to grasp, what was said. But I am not and never have been militarily orientated.

The assistance the Ministry of Defence gave me was most generous and far-reaching, not only with travelling but also in giving me unlimited access to all the soldiers I wanted to talk to, and providing me with totally unsupervised facilities to interview them privately and at length. Entirely voluntarily, I gave an assurance that I would show the MoD the manuscript before publication and discuss anything in it they were unhappy about; and that if there were matters on which we couldn't reach agreement, the right of final veto would be theirs. There were discussions and there were disagreements which we couldn't resolve; but I can only say I'm astonished at how few deletions were finally requested.

During the time I was working on this book I read and enjoyed several others by better-informed writers. Outstanding among them were John Keegan's two near-masterpieces, *The Face of Battle* (Cape 1976) and *Six Armies in Normandy* (Cape 1982). I am very grateful to him too for his advice and assistance in the early stages of my book's preparation. I also found helpful and informative Dennis Barker's *Soldiering On* (André Deutsch 1981), Henry Stanhope's *The Soldiers* (Hamish Hamilton 1979), Michael Barthorp's *Crater to the Creggan* (Leo Cooper 1976), and A. F. N. Clarke's *Contact* (Secker & Warburg 1983). This last, about British soldiers in

Northern Ireland, was most movingly adapted and stunningly filmed for BBC Television by director Alan Clarke. Roger Machell of Hamish Hamilton went to great trouble to find and provide me with a copy of Paul Dehn's poem, and I thank him for that.

Nearly all writers depend heavily on a large group of helpers in the putting-together of a book, and I've been specially fortunate in this. As sole and accurate typist of all the drafts and redrafts of the entire manuscript, Genevieve Broad has responded promptly to every demand both reasonable and unreasonable: to the former always with calm reliability, and to the latter with spirit and good humour. In the early stages Josephine Hugo transcribed and typed out lengthy personal-note cassettes: in later ones Vivien Broad made numerous car journeys in freezing weather to ensure work was delivered or collected. The lovely Rose Tremain and the loving and lovable John Dudley made regular and enlivening guest-appearances in my life that cheered and encouraged me; and Ruth Whittaker wrote me poems that I carried with me and read from time to time almost everywhere I went. I thank them all, not only for all they did, but for always being as they are: my friends. I am indebted too to Group Management Services of Halesworth for so speedily and efficiently providing me with carefully reproduced and collated copies of the manuscript. My agent Anthony Sheil was, as ever, supportive, protective and helpful with advice; and David Godwin of Heinemann was a pleasure to work for, and constantly understanding.

Nothing at all that I could say could be even remotely adequate to express my thanks to my wife Margery. Her assistance in every way has been selfless and enormous. Without her I should never have completed the book, and that is no mere formal acknowledgment of her contribution but a plain statement of fact. Her practical assistance has been endless, and her love and support cannot ever in any way be properly repaid.

                                                            Tony Parker

Westleton, Suffolk

D1388947